Floriana Petersen

111 Places
in Silicon Valley
That You Must
Not Miss

Photographs by Steve Werney

emons:

© Emons Verlag GmbH
All rights reserved
© Photographs: Steve Werney
Art Credits: Pace Gallery (ch. 48): Continues Life and Death in the
Now of Eternity by TeamLab; Palo Alto Public Art Tour (ch. 51):
Tilted Donut No. 5, 2005, Fletcher Benton/Artist Rights Society (ARS)
New York; Falafel's Drive In (ch. 66): Lila Gemellos; MACLA (ch. 71):
Walls Can't Keep Out Greatness by Jessica Sabogal; Playa To Paseo (ch. 74):
XO by Laura Kimpton with Jeff Schomberg; Victory Stand (ch. 79):
Rigo 23; Triton Art Museum (ch. 89): Triton by Alexandrovich Schnittmann;
Libby's Water Tank (ch. 104): Anita Kaplan; Djerassi Foundation Artist
Program (ch. 107): Vanishing Ship by John Roloff
© Cover motif: shutterstock.com/Robert Lucian Crusitu
Layout: Eva Kraskes, based on a design
by Lübbeke | Naumann | Thoben
Edited by Karen E. Seiger
Maps: altancicek.design, www.altancicek.de
Basic cartographical information from Openstreetmap,
© OpenStreetMap-Mitwirkende, ODbL
Printing and binding: Lensing Druck GmbH & Co. KG,
Feldbachacker 16, 44149 Dortmund
Printed in Germany 2019
ISBN 978-3-7408-0493-0
First edition

Did you enjoy this guidebook? Would you like to see more?
Join us in uncovering new places around the world on:
www.111places.com

Foreword

When I first moved to San Francisco from Slovenia, a friend from Palo Alto took me to Filoli and its spacious gardens. The Filoli estate and those spectacular grounds amazed me because they were so evocative of 19th-century Italian designs. My daughter Adriana has always gravitated to the gardens as well, and all these years later, we still find refuge in that serenity.

The history that we discovered at Filoli led us to other gardens and estates on the peninsula, Hakone gardens and Villa Montalvo. We were always on the trail of whatever was blooming. As my life in this new country continued, new trails opened up to me. I discovered Castle Rock and the many trail systems along the golden hills. I also discovered that under the suburban sprawl of office parks and expressways, there were art collections as rich and varied as those of metropolitan cities, like Pace Gallery and many other venues waiting to be discovered. I love looking under the layers to find new favorites, such as MACLA in San José.

And then there is the heartbreaking story of 15-year-old Leland Stanford Jr., the namesake of the university, whose drawings, you can find on campus at the Cantor Arts Center. I became interested in how that tragedy became such a catalyst for academic achievement, and also for Silicon Valley as we know it today. This line of thought leads to the Resident Artists Program at the Djerassi Ranch. Carl Djerassi was the Stanford chemist who developed the birth control pill. In 1978, his daughter Pamela, a painter and poet, died. He saw her death as "a message to survivors" and created one of the great artist colonies in America. The revelation I had while writing this book is the extent to which Silicon Valley is so intricately and elaborately connected through the human experience, and largely, although not entirely, for the benefit of mankind.

I hope this guidebook will help tell the full story of this fascinating, ever-evolving valley, which I feel lucky to have explored so deeply.

111 Places

1 Atherton

Putting the haute in prestige

The life of Faxon Dean Atherton is hardly known. He was born in Massachusetts in 1815, became an entrepreneur in Valparaiso, Chile trading hides and foodstuffs, and eventually found his way to Northern California. He became a very wealthy man and owned property in what is now San Mateo County until his death in 1877. In 1923, when town elders were looking to incorporate and couldn't use the existing name of Fair Oaks, as it was already taken, they chose Atherton.

It's now a rectangular space, population 7,300, south of Redwood City, between Highways 101 and 280. Best known for its warren of curvy lanes, the town is lined with oaks. The town describes itself as "a scenic, rural, thickly wooded residential area with abundant open space," not to mention home to a collection of Eichler houses and The Menlo Circus Club, the definitive Silicon Valley country club, the Menlo Polo Club (since 1923), and the fairly unknown, diamond-shaped Arthur Mathews House, hidden behind the old oak trees, designed in 1950 by Frank Lloyd Wright. It's also where Eric Schmidt (Google), Sheryl Sandberg (Facebook), and Meg Whitman (HP), among others, call home, and the former home of baseball legend Willie Mays.

Atherton is the most affluent zip code in the country year after year, driven largely by the tech wealth, but also increasingly by Indian and Chinese investors looking for arguably the most prestigious address in Silicon Valley. They often pay cash, sometimes for mansions unseen. In the last few years, brokers report a frenzy of interest for homes in Atherton costing $10 million or more.

There is charming and quaint Atherton train station located on One Dinkelspiel Station Lane, where trains stop at the station just on the weekends, and train operators have to follow the 'quiet zone' rule, where they may only blow their horns when they encounter a hazard.

Address Atherton, CA 94027, www.ci.atherton.ca.us | Getting there Caltrain to Atherton, or ECR bus towards 1000 El Camino Real-Menlo College, or El Camino Real & 5th Avenue | Hours Unrestricted | Tip Holbrook-Palmer Park, Atherton's central park and recreational area, is a 22-acre, tree-covered park, with tennis courts, a playground, gardens, and walking paths (150 Watkins Avenue, Atherton, CA 94027, www.ci.atherton.ca.us/180/Holbrook---Palmer-Park).

2 Menlo Circus Club

Where they play 'the game of kings'

You turn off El Camino Real and go down country lanes lined with soft shoulders, thick hedges, and formidable gates. Eventually, you reach one of the valley's true inner sanctums, the Menlo Circus Club. It's private of course, hidden away in a neighborhood reminiscent in spirit of Fitzgerald's West Egg, thick with local Gatsbys and Atherton blue bloods. The lore is that in the summer of 1920, a muster of young girls banded together to present a homemade circus to entertain their parents. The children brought horses and ponies, as well as goats and cats, along with dogs they had trained to do tricks.

The first circus was held on Middlefield Road on fields behind the home of Mrs. W. B. Weir, who proposed that the event raise money for the local convalescent home, now the Lucile Packard Children's Hospital. The 'circus' was a roaring success, socially above all, and became a local tradition – so much so that in 1922, neighbors purchased several hundred acres and incorporated the Menlo Circus Club. A century later the club's equestrian center is unmatched, with climate-controlled, 12-foot-by-12-foot stalls and windows front and back, along with blacksmith bays, tack rooms, and grooming stalls.

The real equestrian nature of the club has always been linked to polo, which has been described as like "playing golf in an earthquake." The game, played on an area the size of nine football fields, sets two teams of four against each other. There are four or eight seven-minute periods, or chukkers. Riders swap horses at the end of each chukker or else in the middle. The horses are specially trained to wheel, sprint, and stop on a dime, racing back and forth at up to 35 miles an hour. The best polo ponies are distinguished by soft mouths that make them easier to control. Catch a match during polo season at the club (18 through September 30, no matches in August).

Address 190 Park Lane, Atherton, CA 94027, +1 (650)322-4616, www.menlocircusclub.com, jasona@menlocircusclub.com | Getting there Caltrain to Atherton, then ECR bus to 1000 El Camino Real-Menlo College | Hours Visit website for polo play times and other club activities | Tip Stop by Allied Arts Guild, an historic Spanish-Colonial-style complex and garden created to host artists' studios, unique shops, and the Blue Garden Café (75 Arbor Road, Menlo Park, CA 94025, www.alliedartsguild.org).

3__Music at Menlo

For connoisseurs of chamber music

In the new world of classical music, big-city symphonies remain largely successful. The San Francisco Symphony is a bright, shining example. What's changing is music programming and new donor patterns. Unlike the old days, Silicon Valley philanthropists give money with strings attached and expect results.

The other great change in classical music is the venue. The concert hall is downsizing. The reason is that the 110-piece orchestra, that performance dreadnaught, is giving way to the 4-, 10-, or 20-member ensembles, which find their audiences at festivals. The Bay Area offers several high-quality classical music festivals, from Napa to Santa Cruz to Carmel. But there's one particularly impressive annual chamber music festival in Menlo Park in the heart of Silicon Valley.

Menlo School is a private prep school founded in 1915 that has a state-of-the-art concert hall center for performing arts, as well an exquisite chamber music hall. It is home to Music@Menlo, which hosts resident artist concerts year-round and even a music travel program with unique musical experiences worldwide. The school is also the place where Music@Menlo Festival takes place.

Music@Menlo, a three-week affair in July, was started in 2003 by two musicians, cellist David Finckel and his wife, pianist Wu Han. They're two of the most honored and entrepreneurial people in the chamber music world, and have turned their business model into a way to spread 'chamber music startups' across the country. In addition to Menlo, they oversee the Chamber Music Society of Lincoln Center, the Saratoga Performing Arts Center Festival, and a festival in Seoul. Menlo festival artists include rising stars such as pianist Michael Brown and violinist Paul Huang. The festival also includes lectures, given by people like violist Paul Neubauer and Ara Guzelimian, dean of the Juilliard School.

Address Menlo School, 50 Valparaiso Avenue, Atherton, CA 94027, +1 (650)330-2030, www.musicatmenlo.org, info@musicatmenlo.org | **Getting there** Bus 82, 83, 84 to Valparaiso Avenue & University Drive | **Hours** See website for performance times | **Tip** TheatreWorks Silicon Valley hosts a rich schedule of theater, ballet, and musicals (500 Castro Street, Mountain View, CA 94041, www.theatreworks.org).

4__ Water Dog Lake
Don't forget your Ovilus

Belmont is a town of less than 30,000, halfway between San Francisco and Santa José. It's the home of Oracle, Safeway, and a small Catholic university. Among the town's several recreational areas is Water Dog Lake Park, which you'll find off Ralston Avenue. There is a good trailhead from which to reach the lake on Lyall Street. The walk to the lake winds along a firebreak, up a slope that will make you and your dog pant. But the name 'water dog' actually refers to a type of salamander, also called a mudpuppy or a waterdog, that make barking sounds. Note the sign warning of rattlesnakes and mountain lions.

The place is quiet, located in a canyon surrounded by native oaks and California buckeyes. It is popular among local dog owners, mountain bikers, and hikers who enjoy a number of secluded trails. The lake is really a small reservoir, built by William Ralston as a source of water for the Ralston Mansion, nowadays situated on the campus of Notre Dame de Namur University. The intricate pipe system was finished in 1874.

The urban legend here is that the lake is haunted by the ghost of a little boy from the area who went to the park, disappeared, and was murdered. The bones of the story are true. In early October in 1984, a 12-year-old boy drifted away from his soccer practice and went to nearby Water Dog Lake Park. When he didn't return home that evening, his parents called the police, and that night the boy's body was found near the lake. The murderer was a 23-year-old serial killer, who was eventually indicted for three murders and sent to California's death row in 1990.

The haunting continues to draw interest from the likes of self-described paranormal investigators, such as Keith Weldon, who tours the lake with a cameraman and a ghost-busting device, the Ghost Box Ovilus III, which he claims can "convert environmental readings into real words."

Address 2400 Lyall Way, Belmont, CA 94002, www.bahiker.com/southbayhikes/waterdog.html | Getting there Bus 60, 62, 260 to Continentals Way & Lyall Way | Hours Daily dawn–dusk | Tip In the small mall just down the street, you'll find Ladera Garden & Gifts, where you can pick up greenery, flowers, and decorative items to freshen up your home (Carlmont Village Shopping Center, 2029 Ralston Avenue, Belmont, CA 94002, www.laderagardenandgifts.com).

5__ The Van's Restaurant
Down home on the Hill

In Belmont, there's a getaway restaurant up on a hill above El Camino Real called The Van's. It's not Van's, but The Van's, and not well known except by regulars, and older regulars at that. They come for the Southern fried sirloin strip steak, "draped" with country gravy, or else chicken livers, sautéed with mushrooms, onions and white wine. Patrons also come for the 180-degree view, which on a clear day, extends to the East Bay. Or, they come to sit in one of the valley's most intimate little sports bars, which caters to 49er and Giants fans. Take out is available.

The restaurant has enormous early 20th-century charm and is an unofficial historical site. The restaurant is in a building built for the Japanese Exhibition at the Panama Pacific International Exposition in 1915, still featuring original, lightly faded alizarin red wallpaper with Chinese figurines in yellow ink in the dining room. The bar décor is original, with upper walls surrounded with the dark wood cut panels portraying San Francisco in its early days.

The Exposition was San Francisco's way of assuring the world that it had fully recovered from the horrors of 1906. The buildings for the exposition were designed to come down after it closed, which was in keeping with Richard Maybeck's notion that every city should have some ruins. His Palace of Fine Arts was left in ruins but was rebuilt in the 1960s.

Two other buildings also survived, one at Civic Center, the Bill Graham Civic Auditorium, across from the library, and the Japanese Tea House, which was disassembled and barged down the bay to Belmont at the pleasure of a land baron named E. D. Swift. In 1933, an entrepreneur named Elsie Smuck brought the place, and during Prohibition, 'Elsie's' became a private, three-story refuge for those interested in booze, broads, and dice. In 1947 the place became The Van's.

Address 815 Belmont Avenue, Belmont, CA 94002, +1 (650)591-6525, www.thevansrestaurant.com | **Getting there** Bus 62, 68 to El Camino Real & Davey Glen Road | **Hours** Mon–Fri 11:30am–10pm, Sat & Sun 4–10pm | **Tip** Twin Paines is a lovely park with a creek and many trees, hidden behind the Belmont City Hall (1 Twin Pines Lane, Belmont, CA 94002).

6_ Esalen Institute

Where techies reboot

The hot springs at Esalen, a few miles south of the Henry Miller Library in Big Sur, drew the attention of local Native Americans in approximately 2600 **B.C.** In the late 19th century, a fellow named Thomas Slate founded a small settlement on the spot. Nearly a century after that, in the 1960s, The Esalen Institute was founded as "a leading center for exploring and realizing human potential through experience, education, and research." Joan Baez lived in a cabin on the property, and 'gonzo' journalist Hunter S. Thompson briefly managed the place. Author Henry Miller also lived close by, and noted in his book, *Big Sur and the Oranges of Hieronymus Bosch*, that this particular paradise, meaning the expanse of Big Sur in general, doesn't suit everyone.

Critics of Esalen dismiss it as the Oz of touchy-feely or else question its corporatization. Proponents point to the illuminati who have always come to Esalen, from Joseph Campbell to Robert Reich.

This holistic notion has had increasing appeal for the gold barons of the era, whose industry has recently been caught up in a series of sex and political scandals and, worse, calls for regulation.

Ben Tauber, the executive director at Esalen and a former product manager at Google, once charged with improving Google Hangouts and other social products, has been quoted as saying, "There's a dawning consciousness emerging in Silicon Valley as people recognize that their conventional success isn't necessarily making the world a better place. The CEOs, inside they're hurting. They can't sleep at night." One of the courses offered at Esalen addresses 'Depression and Tech.'

There are other similar centers, such as 1440 Multiversity near Santa Cruz. The goal is to "recognize that the blazing success of the Internet catalyzed powerful connections, yet did not help people connect to themselves."

Address Esalen Institute, 55000 CA-1, Big Sur, CA 93920, +1 (831)667-3000, www.esalen.org, info@easalen.org | Getting there By car only, take CA-1 to the institute | Hours Visit the website for accommodation and classes | Tip Stop by at the Henry Miller Memorial Library and browse the bookstore, dedicated to the late American writer and former Big Sur resident (48603 Highway One, Big Sur, CA 93920, www.henrymiller.org).

7___It's It Ice Cream Factory

Sweet dreams between two cookies

There is no one, agreed-upon definition of a startup. Some insist it's merely a state of mind designed to accommodate the creative instincts of people under 40. Or else it's the desire to take risks in the 'culture of wow.' In fact, there are certain common characteristics of a startup: Internet scalability, the ability to secure venture capital or crowdfunding, and a nimble staff of coders and marketers working in a casual atmosphere to combine disruption with innovation. And do it all quickly.

In that sense, the entrepreneurial spirit of Silicon Valley is unique, or it was until it became so widely duplicated. But you could argue that this spirit has long distinguished the area, beginning with businesses generated after the Gold Rush. Boudin's sourdough bread comes to mind. And speaking of food, consider George Whitney, a San Francisco businessman in the mid-1920s who once, on a visit to Morro Bay, came across a market that sold ice cream and freshly baked cookies. Locals sometimes asked that the ice cream be put between the cookies like a sandwich. Whitney wondered what would happen if you dipped the sandwich in chocolate. A sweet sensation was born.

Whitney opened an ice cream shop in San Francisco at Playlands, the legendary amusement spark and rode his success until Playlands closed in 1972. Two years later, the business changed hands and was eventually bought by the four Shamieh brothers. They solicited crowdfunding from family and private investors and opened a factory in Burlingame, where they could automate the process of dipping the ice cream sandwiches in chocolate. Forty years later, very much in the spirit of a startup, It's It does no advertising and sells millions of their products every year, mostly ice cream sandwiches. You can buy them in supermarkets, corner stores, order them online, or visit their factory store.

Address 865 Burlway Road, Burlingame, CA 94010, +1 (800)345-1928, www.itsiticecream.com | Getting there Bus 292 to Bayshore Highway & Burlway Road | Hours Mon–Fri 10am–5:30pm | Tip For even more ice cream, the Museum of Ice Cream in San Francisco offers "an immersive tasting experience, uniting the world through ice cream" (1 Grant Avenue, San Francisco, CA 94108, www.museumoficecream.com/san-francisco).

8__ The PEZ Museum

From tchotchkes to 'bad toys'

In 1927, a wealthy Austrian inventor named Eduard Haas III developed the first breath mint, which he imagined might help break the smoking habit. Twenty years later, he invented a plastic dispenser in the shape of the cigarette lighter filled with peppermint-flavored candies. PEZ is an acronym taken from the German, *pfefferminze*. The dispenser is distinguished by the spring-loaded character heads. In the 1960s, PEZ heads included Disney characters, and these days, Star Wars figures. In 1952, Haas opened a subsidiary in America that continues to produce new flavors and designs, all with cultural echoes. New designs come out every month, and with popularity has come collector conventions, auctions, and a museum.

The world's only known PEZ museum is located on a side street in Burlingame. The museum is two blocks from the train station in a two-room former computer repair shop. In the front room, walls are filled with Pez figures, including all the 800 unique dispensers made since 1950, including an 8-foot-tall PEZ dispenser in the shape of a snowman that dispenses other PEZ dispensers. In the back room is the museum. A 15-minute tour is $3 and given by Gary Doss, proprietor and PEZ aficionado, who 20 years ago decided to close his computer store to open the PEZ Museum. You can also buy discontinued and new PEZ dispensers, as well as entire collections.

The museum features not only all things PEZ, including Mr. Doss' favorite, the Psychedelic Eye, but also an issue of the first comic book, early incarnations of erector sets, Lincoln Logs, and a Mr. Potato Head. But the hallmark of the museum is most certainly the 'banned toys,' or as Mr. Doss puts it, "bad toys." These include very sharp steel lawn darts, a 1951 Atomic Energy Laboratory complete with radioactive material, and a Teletubby who seems to be saying, "Bite my butt."

Address 214 California Drive, Burlingame, CA 94010, +1 (650)347-2301, www.burlingamepezmuseum.com, garydosspez@yahoo.com | **Getting there** Caltrain to Burlingame | **Hours** Tue–Sat 10am–6pm | **Tip** The Burlingame train station is actually quite fascinating. Built in 1894 in the Spanish-Colonial-revival style, it's listed as a California Historical Landmark (290 California Drive, Burlingame, CA 94010, www.caltrain.com/stations/burlingamestation.html).

9___ The Sawyer Camp Segment

Riding the San Andreas Fault line

The Crystal Springs Reservoir is set in the San Andreas Fault Rift Valley and stretches forseventeen-and-a-half miles along the western edge of I-280 in San Mateo County, providing an unexpected wilderness backdrop for daily commuters from San Francisco to Silicon Valley. This recognized Biosphere Reserve not only protects Bay Area drinking water but also provides habitat for more than 180 bird species. And about halfway down the trail is the Jepson Laurel Tree, a California bay laurel that's at least 600 years old, reputedly the oldest laurel in the state. The fragrance of bay laurel permeates the area, and the picnic area here is a great place for lunch.

When pioneer Leander Sawyer first came to the area around Crystal Springs in 1853 – nearly a century after that relentless explorer Gaspar de Portola camped here – Sawyer did what settlers have been doing ever since: he found a source of water and built a small adobe house nearby. He also built a small inn along the stagecoach line running between Millbrae and Half Moon Bay. He became a hotelier for travelers and kept cattle partly to keep roads open to wagons.

Today, the Peninsula Watershed, especially around Sawyer Camp Segment of the Crystal Springs Regional Trail, is a sort of outdoor workout space for valley techies. The trail has been paved with a painted line to distinguish North- and South-bound traffic. It can be busy on weekends, with a promenade of cyclists, runners, and walkers. All the while you may wonder at the state of things underneath you, on the most iconic fault line in California. It turns out the plates in the fault are moving horizontally not vertically, so you need not worry that California will splinter and fall into the ocean. However, you can ponder a recent prediction that there is a 99.7 percent chance of a magnitude 6.7 earthquake or larger along the fault by 2037.

Address 950 Skyline Boulevard, Burlingame, CA 94010, parks.smcgov.org/sawyer-camp-segment | **Getting there** By car, take I-280 to Skyline Boulevard | **Hours** Daily dawn–dusk | **Tip** From I-280, just across from Sawyer Park, you can see the famous Flintstone House, a single-family home built in the 1970. It contains several domes and is surrounded by large sculptures of dinosaurs, wooly mammoths, and a giraffe.

10 Los Gatos Creek Trail

A good dog's life

The corporate strategy for maximizing productivity in Silicon Valley has long been to make the workplace feel like home, thus fewer reasons to go home. Many companies offer exotic sports facilities, hip cultural activities, campus social life, and even transportation. Google, for example, runs employee busses between San Francisco and Mountain View. Some busses even cater to workers bringing their pets.

Such is the growing 'pet perk.' Think of pets, particularly dogs, as antidotes to the seemingly emotionless culture of code. Google has a code of conduct and pet policy: "Google's affection for our canine friends is an integral facet of our corporate culture." Under Google's policy, pets can roam as they please, but if they have more than one indoor 'accident,' they will be asked to go home. Moreover, owners are responsible for "cleaning up excessive pet hair and odor removal."

Los Gatos Creek County Park, which features an exciting, 11-mile trail that blends city and country views, has become a favorite of dog walkers (only a little ironic, given the park's name). There is also a separate dog park along the trail that features two fenced-in areas, one for big dogs, the other for small.

Zynga has a 'barking lot' next to their main entrance, along with a comprehensive pet policy that honors cats, rabbits, lizards, and ferrets. MWare has more than 90 dogs registered to visit their company. Amazon, in Seattle, has 4,000 registered dogs. Kimpton Hotels, one of the first to encourage dogs in the workplace, offers pet insurance that includes pet bereavement leave.

The new company status for dogs, helped by the likes of Mark Zuckerberg's Beast, a Hungarian sheepdog, who has 2.6 million Facebook followers, has led urban planners to create more parks for dogs. Valley favorites also include Butcher Dog Park in San José and Rengstorff Park in Mountain View.

Address 1250 Dell Avenue, Campbell, CA 95008, +1 (408)793-5510, www.losgatosca.gov/907/Los-Gatos-Creek-Trail | Getting there Light rail 902 to Winchester, walk 17 minutes west to Dell Avenue | Hours Daily dawn–dusk | Tip Visit Testarossa Winery, also in Los Gatos, the fourth oldest continuously operating winery in California (300 College Avenue, Los Gatos, www.testarossa.com).

11 Apple Headquarters

Close encounters of the Jobs kind

The highly anticipated Apple Headquarters opened in 2017 at 1 Apple Park Way in Cupertino. Ring shaped and nicknamed 'The Spaceship,' the four-story building and campus rest on 175 acres. It looks like a super-sized sports stadium, or even a 21st-century castle – there's an Arthurian quality to its spirit. The building is one mile in circumference and 2.8 million square feet and features a 1,000-seat auditorium. The campus cost $5 billion and accommodates 12,000 employees.

It all began in the mind of Steve Jobs (see ch. 41), the infinitely precise creative who believed form follows function in all things. "His vision for Apple Park was to create an incredible workplace for the future. Where engineers and designers could all be together, collaborating on the next generation of Apple product to change the world," said Apple CEO Tim Cook.

For the park, every design detail is accounted for, down to the elevator buttons, the undersides of stairs, the plant boxes in the atriums, the Louis Vuitton, high-grade leather office chairs, and the gray Apple bikes used to get around the campus. Unfortunately, Apple Park is not open to the public.

Ironically, the walls are glass, which suggests a transparency that doesn't exist. It's just not part of the Silicon Valley ethos, for obvious reasons. Silicon Valley is all about the value of secrets. Instagram photos taken by employees of the interior of the park were taken down. "We didn't make Apple Park for other people," Apple's chief design officer Sir Jonathan Ive was quoted as saying in 2018.

However, there is a visitor center across from the ring, which includes a store (without a genius bar), a café, and an augmented reality (AR) exhibit that shows the park through a drone's eye. The rooftop area offers a tantalizing view of the ring – if only it were just a little higher so you could see inside…

Address Apple Park Visitor Center, 10600 North Tantau Avenue, Cupertino, CA 95014, +1 (408)961-1560, www.apple.com/retail/appleparkvisitorcenter | **Getting there** VTA bus 81 to Tantau & Prune Ridge | **Hours** Mon–Fri 9am–7pm, Sat 10am–7pm, Sun 11am–6pm | **Tip** A mile away is Cupertino Memorial Park, a nice place to stroll or read a book next to the pond and a playground. Look for the Guardian Statue in the Cupertino Veterans Memorial with likenesses of two local Navy SEALS who died in action (21121 Stevens Creek Boulevard, Cupertino, CA 95014, www.cupertinoveteransmemorial.org).

12 Bigfoot Discovery Museum
Among the new normals, the paranormal

In an era when popular conviction trumps trust in the scientific method and data, superstitions appear ever more credible. A 2018 Chapman University study found that around 20 percent of Americans believe that the Big Bang is as real as Bigfoot. Moreover, the number of people who believe in Bigfoot has increased markedly in the last five years. By one count, always open to authentication, there have been nearly 450 Bigfoot sightings in California in the last century, including sightings in the Lake Tahoe area, Humboldt County, and in the Santa Cruz Mountains around the town of Felton.

Felton is a town of 4,000 in the San Lorenzo Valley, just north of Santa Cruz. It's best known as a gateway to the Henry Cowell Redwoods State Park, for a narrow-gauge railroad attraction, and for the CapriTaurus Bigfoot Discovery Museum on Highway 9 just south of downtown.

The two-room museum is a haven for those drawn to movie clips and footprint casts, with an extensive library, Bigfoot merchandise, and a map of Bigfoot sightings since the early 1900s. But the revelation here is talking with Mike Rugg, who claims to have seen a Bigfoot creature when he was five and has been a hobbyist ever since. He graduated from Stanford and worked as a computer programmer. But after the bubble burst in 2000, he felt that the future of the valley was the younger generation's and moved to Felton to open a museum, where he could live and educate.

Over the years, Mr. Rugg has become a celebrity in Big Foot culture. For example, you can hear him in a famous 2011 Bigfoot Tonight radio show being interviewed by the late Bigfoot authority Chuck Prahl. Rugg is also an expert on The Sasquatch Genome Project, whose DNA analysis supports the notion of an unknown hominid in the United States that is a hybrid with a human mother and a father of non-human but unknown origin.

Address 5497 Highway 9, Felton, CA 95018, +1 (831)335-4478, www.bigfootdiscoveryproject.com | Getting there Bus 35A to Graham Hill Road & Highway 9 | Hours Wed–Mon 11am–6pm | Tip In Felton, you can hop on century-old steam locomotives for an old-fashioned ride into glorious redwood country (5401 Graham Hill Road, Felton, CA 95018, www.roaringcamp.com).

13_Foster City

Where the blue waters flow

Foster City is located by the South Bay on the periphery of Silicon Valley. It is a planned suburban community built on landfill at the western approaches to the San Mateo Bridge, which runs across the bay to Hayward and beyond. It's named after T. Jack Foster, who bought Brewer Island – which consisted of four square miles of dairy farms and salt ponds – for $200,000 in 1958. Foster dredged the wetlands for six years to form 230 acres of lagoons and pumped 18 million cubic yards of mud and sand onto the island, raising it slightly above sea level.

Snake-shaped canals and lagoons, which are lined with homes whose backyards often include a small dock and a patio overlooking the water, are the trademark of Foster City, a town with 30,000 residents boasting less than one murder per decade. The city injects up to 150 gallons of nontoxic dye into the water each month from April to October to block ultraviolet light, thus preventing the growth of algae, and particularly the widgeon grass, that might otherwise entangle sailboat rudders, paddle boarders, and swimmers. Hence, the color of the water is always vibrant cerulean. The canals are about six feet deep, and the depth is controlled by pumps.

The area includes a number of parks. On Wednesday nights from March through October, Leo Ryan Park hosts 'Off the Grid' events with food trucks. On Friday evenings there is live music at the Leo Ryan Park Amphitheater. Shorebird Park offers access to the Bay Trail, a favorite walk for locals that is also enjoyed by cyclists, runners, and all kinds of athletes. The levee is also very popular for windsurfing, kayaking, and other water sports. There is a section of the Shells Beach with a pathway through a forest of tall grass that takes you to the Shells Dirt Jumps with dunes made from piles of solidified dirt and salt that attracts and encourages all kinds of bicyclists to catch some air.

Address Foster City, CA 94404, www.fostercity.org | Getting there Bus 54, 251 to Shell Boulevard & East Hillsdale Boulevard | Hours Unrestricted | Tip Visit Foster City Recreation Center for information about the outdoor activities in the area (650 Shell Boulevard, Foster City, CA 94404, www.fostercity.org/parksrec).

14_ Children's Natural History Museum

Tales of the 'Boy Paleontologists'

Fremont, which lies along the eastern frontier of Silicon Valley, was formed in 1956 from a handful of townships. One of these was Irvington, then an out-of-the-way intersection known to locals as Four Corners. It was also known in the 1940s and 1950s for its quarries, particularly Bell Quarry, now submerged under a freeway. It turned out that this quarry was rich with geological treasure, including rare fossils from large woolly mammoths, great mastodons, giant sloths, saber-toothed Smilodons, ancient horses, and camelops, unusually large camels that plied through western North America. Mostly from the Pleistocene ecosystem, the fossils around Irvington were so enlightening that a whole period in geological history is named the Irvingtonian Era.

The fossils were discovered in 1867 by an amateur paleontologist named Lorenzo Yates. But it was in the 1940s that Wes Gordon, a teacher in the local school system, brought the local fossils to public attention. Gordon was a one-time pastor who became drawn to paleontology and enlisted more than a dozen students, mostly boys but some girls. A *Life Magazine* article in 1944 cast them as the 'Boy Paleontologists.' During the 1940s and 1950s, Gordon's little band met every Saturday and dug up some 20,000 fossils representing 58 discrete animal species – all this from local creeks and the quarry. The bounty was taken to UC Berkeley, but there was so much that Gordon eventually opened a museum in a local school, which evolved into the Children's Natural History Museum.

The museum, now under the broad umbrella of the Math / Science Nucleus, features a planetarium, microscopes with microfossils to look at along with bones and shells, and an exhibit about the budding scientists who found them.

Address 4074 Eggers Drive, Fremont, CA 94536, +1 (510)790-6284, www.cnhm.msnucleus.org | **Getting there** Bus 99 to Fremont Boulevard & Eggers Drive | **Hours** Tue & Thu 2–5pm, first & third Sat 1–5pm | **Tip** Visit Ardenwood Historic Farm, which still grows produce using practices from over 100 years ago (34600 Ardenwood Boulevard, Fremont, CA 94555, www.ebparks.org/parks/ardenwood).

15_Mission Peak

Hang gliding in heaven

The Diablo Mountain Range forms the eastern border of Silicon Valley. It's part of the geological system of coastal ranges in this part of California, and propelled upward by pressure from the Calaveras Fault to the east and the Hayward Fault to the west. The range includes several peaks, including Mission Peak, which rises to 2,520 feet above Fremont. The landscape is distinguished by rolling hills, valleys, and plateaus, along with Tule elk, black-tailed deer, vultures, and coyotes. Northern Pacific rattlesnakes thrive here. Although largely barren, there are shaded areas along with chaparral and California oak, some of which are up to 600 years old.

The peak is part of a regional preserve with two popular access points, one at Ohlone College, the other from Stanford Avenue. The preserve has become an increasingly popular site. On weekends, between 1,500 and 2,000 people a day make the six-mile pilgrimage up to the summit. The views are as you might imagine: on a clear day you can see forever. The hike takes between two and five hours.

Mission Peak is also a popular launch spot for hang gliding and paragliding. In 1971, a daredevil named Dave Kilbourne (d. 2011) flew off Mission Ridge in a flexwing hang glider. He took off without assistance and was the first in the world to do so. He flew for an hour and established Mission Peak as a glider venue. He also founded The Wings of Rogallo Northern California Hang Gliding Association, which has been licensed by the East Bay Regional Park District since 1983 to administer the sport. All pilots must have an association membership along with an advanced USHPA rating for either paragliding or hang gliding. You can watch takeoffs from the launch point up toward the ridge and marked by a large windsock. Landings are along the main hiking trail about one quarter mile from the Stanford Avenue entrance.

Address Parking Ohlone College, 43600 Mission Boulevard, Fremont, CA 94539, www.ebparks.org/parks/mission/default.htm | Getting there BART to Warm Springs/ South Fremont (Orange Line), then bus 239 to Mission Boulevard/Grimmer Boulevard, walk 0.8 miles to Stanford Avenue Staging Area | Hours Dec 23–Mar 31, daily 6:30am–8pm; Apr 1–Dec 22, daily 6:30am–9pm | Tip The history of Fremont is captured in the displays at the small Museum of Local History (190 Anza Street, Fremont, CA 94539, www.museumoflocalhistory.org).

16 Mission San José
A self-sustaining village

As every California fourth grader learns, the coastal cities of the state were founded by Catholic missionaries walking slowly northward from what is now Mexico. Of course, in 1797, California was Mexico. Or at least the Spanish thought so. No one asked the Ohlone, the indigenous people of Santa Clara County, who had long populated villages along the bay, including one in what is now Fremont. The Ohlone called it Oroysom.

In an area that has always known boom and bust, the arrival of the missionaries – from the native perspective – was a bust. Within a few generations of their arrival, the native population was dramatically reduced through disease and cultural disruption. Nevertheless, the names, the gardens, and the distinctive architecture brought by the missionaries became the pattern for the many settlements of California.

Mission San José's main building, a two-story, white adobe structure rebuilt in 1985, replicates the original, which was destroyed by an earthquake in 1868. The thick adobe walls are supported by heavy buttresses on one side and a bell tower on the other. The inside of the chapel is restored with hand-painted walls and an open-beam ceiling, contrasting with the ornate altar. The chapel is still an active Catholic church. The grounds, restored in 1985, provide a clear glimpse into mission living; note the museum, housed in one of the original buildings. Among the artifacts on display are musical instruments once played by the resident Ohlone choir and orchestra, who were famous throughout California.

In 1833, when Mexico decided to secularize the lands owned by the church and divide them into *ranchos,* the era of the missions ended. When the westward land boom began, the discovery of a cross-country route by John C. Frémont, otherwise known as The Pathfinder, passing below nearby Mission Peak, gave the city its current name.

Address 43300 Mission Boulevard, Fremont, CA 94539, +1 (510)657-1797, www.missionsanjose.org | **Getting there** From Fremont BART station, take bus 217 to Mission Boulevard & Washington Boulevard | **Hours** Daily 10am–5pm | **Tip** Across the street is the small but wonderful Olive Hyde Art Gallery representing local artists (123 Washington Boulevard, Fremont, www.missionsanjose.org).

17_Niles Essanay Silent Film Museum

"Action" in the silent film era

The Essanay silent film studio took off in Chicago in 1907. The name was derived from the last names of the two founders: Spoor, a financier, and Anderson, an actor who became known as Bronco Billy. Essanay's first film, *An Awful Skate* or *The Hobo on Rollers*, starred the company janitor, a burlesque comedian named Ben Turpin whose signature was his cross-eyed stare. When silent film scripts turned to Westerns, Essanay looked for new studio locations, first in Colorado, Santa Barbara, Los Angeles, and finally in Niles, a billiard pocket of a town 20 miles east of San José, up against the foothills of the Diablo mountains.

Essanay struck gold with several actors, including Wallace Beery and Gloria Swanson, but above all with Charlie Chaplin, the enigmatic comedian, who spent a year with Essanay, doing seven films in the first three months of 1915 and then releasing one each month after that – fourteen films in total. These were among his early works, which include the *Little Tramp* series, and suggest his growing sense as actor, writer, and director. This was also when he fell in love with Olga Purviance, who became his personal and professional leading lady until 1917.

The historic district of Niles, which is part of Fremont, is best known for the Essanay Silent Film Museum, housed in the Edison Theater, built in 1913 and restored in 2004. In the museum, you can see silent film cameras, projectors, costumes, photographs, and the projection room that lights up with films from the silent film canon most Saturdays and Sundays.

Outside, you are on Niles Boulevard, beneath palm trees and eucalyptus, in a three-block historic district thick with antique stores, a hotel, the train station, Don's Antique Auto Parts, coffee shops, and a biker sports bar.

Address 37417 Niles Boulevard, Fremont, CA 94536, +1 (510)494-1411, www.nilesfilmmuseum.org | Getting there Fremont BART to Niles Boulevard & H Street | Hours Sat & Sun noon–4pm | Tip Just half a mile north is the California Nursery Historic Park, which includes the Vallejo Adobe, built in 1830 (36550 Niles Boulevard, Fremont, CA 94536, www.msnucleus.org/calnursery).

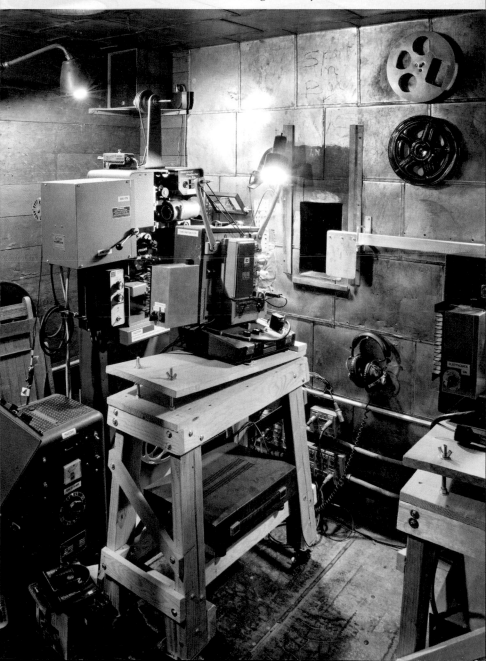

18__ Tesla Factory

Specter of an alien dreadnaught

Among the innovations sprung from the geek-furrowed brows of Silicon Valley engineers is the Tesla mid-sized, all-electric, four-door sedan known as the Model 3. The car, with a range between 220 and 310 miles, began production in July 2017. Tesla produces three models, including the Model 3, which has been developed amid considerable turmoil, especially around production targets. The company is producing nearly 2,500 a week; the hope is to reach 5,000 a week and deliver 220,000 cars annually.

Even if Tesla sold just 100,000 cars, it would be a tremendous achievement in a world where electric vehicles make up less than one percent of the global market. Think of it this way: Tesla would need four more factories running at full capacity to sell just one tenth of what General Motors produced in 2017. Nevertheless, if supply remains uncertain – each car is made to order and takes as long as three months to manufacture – demand is not uncertain. Within 10 days of the unveiling, the number of pre-orders shot above 325,000. The cars are made at a factory in Fremont, otherwise known as Silicon Valley East, a 26-minute drive from the company's headquarters in Palo Alto.

The factory, which employs several thousand workers, has become the economic bedrock of Fremont (Tesla also has a lithium-ion factory in Reno known as the Gigafactory). The Fremont factory, originally a GM-Toyota venture, covers 270 acres and uses so many robots that Tesla CEO Elon Musk admitted he might have put too much trust in automation and not enough on skilled workers. He has likened the factory to an "alien dreadnaught." The company has done much to humanize the space itself though, with skylights, a cafeteria, gym, health center, and patios. Although popular by worker surveys the factory has drawn criticism for a variety of safety issues. Tesla owners are invited to join a factory tour.

Address 45500 Fremont Boulevard, Fremont, CA 94538, +1 (510)249-3500, www.tesla.com/factory, factorytours@teslamotors.com | **Getting there** By car, take I-880 to Fremont Boulevard exit | **Hours** Email to schedule a tour well in advance | **Tip** For adventure types, there is the Secret Sidewalk, a half-buried concrete tunnel of the Spring Valley Aqueduct that runs all the way from Calaveras Reservoir in the East Bay to Fremont (2450 Niles Canyon Road, Fremont, CA 94536).

19 Gilroy Gardens

Trees gone wild

Axel Erlandson (1884–1964) was the son of Swedish American farmers who immigrated to Minnesota in 1886. The boy was obsessed with machines and once built a working reproduction of a thresher. In 1902, the family moved to Hilmar California, an end-of-the-line railway stop in the Central Valley, best known for its evangelical community. The family grew beans, and Axel became interested in inosculation, nature's equivalent of grafting. The phenomenon is most common among plants and trees of the same species.

Erlandson, with his thoughtful expression, often in his fedora and cardigan sweater, was swept away by the possibilities and began grafting, bending, and pruning. He mainly used sycamore trees, designing ladders, hearts, chairs, birdcages, a telephone booth, and a spiral design reminiscent of a double helix. When asked how he was able to do such things with trees, Erlandson answered, "I talk to them." In 1945, he moved his trees to Scotts Valley near Santa Cruz, where people paid good money to visit The Mystery Spot (see ch. 90), a roadside attraction based on a "tilt-induced optical illusion." Axel called the exhibit *The Tree Circus*. For years *Ripley's Believe It or Not!* featured the story.

But Erlandson's *Tree Circus* always seemed plagued by bad luck. As soon as he opened his attraction, a new road, Highway 17, which connected Silicon Valley with Santa Cruz, took business away from Scotts Valley. In 1963, Axel sold the property, which was bought by one developer after another. In 1985, a grocery store magnate and the owner of a tree nursery, bought up 24 of Erlandson's trees and in 2001 opened a family theme park, Gilroy Gardens. It's now owned by the city and has become a popular place to catch gently thrilling rides and Erlandson's Circus Trees. His first creation, the Four Legged Giant, remains alive at the park, probably 80 years or more after it was begun.

Address 3050 Hecker Pass Highway, Gilroy, CA 95020, +1 (408)840-7100, www.gilroygardens.org/play/circus-trees | **Getting there** By car, take US-101 to Masten Avenue. Take exit 360 for Masten Avenue, turn south onto Monterey Road. Turn west on Day Road, and south on Santa Teresa Boulevard, then west on to Hecker Pass Highway. Follow signs to Gilroy Gardens. | **Hours** Fri 11am–5pm, Sat & Sun 10am–6pm | **Tip** Kirigin Cellars Winery is one of the handful of traditional wineries in the area (11550 Watsonville Road, Gilroy, CA 95020, www.kirigincellars.com).

20_ The Carolands

Intimations of American grandeur

Harriet Pullman was the always exquisitely dressed, if melancholy-eyed daughter of George Pullman, who developed the first railway sleeping car. In 1892, Harriet left the East Coast to settle in San Francisco with her husband, Francis Carolan. He owned 550 acres in Hillsborough, 20 miles south of the city, and Harriet, one of the richest women in the world at that time and a devout Francophile, decided that would be the ideal spot to build a 65,000-square-foot American chateau.

She commissioned the notable French architect Ernest Sanson, who offered a design with faint echoes of the Palace of Versailles. The four-and-a-half-story Carolands house includes one hundred rooms, two elevators, nine master bedrooms, endless galleries, and the finest garden. It was largely completed in 1916, the year after Harriet and Frank Carolan divorced. And so began the tortured life of a mansion from the Gilded Age, an encyclopedia of Beaux-Arts architecture that was bought and sold over and over. Little by little, the original property shrank to just five acres. For years, the house was all but abandoned, and some would insist haunted, not least because of the rape and murder of a young woman by a night watchman. But then someone always stepped in to save the place. A local psychiatrist and her husband were the last owners, and in 2012 the house was turned over to a private foundation.

Hillsborough, with its stunning views of the bay, is spread out over the hilly slopes above Burlingame and prides itself on large homes, but Carolands is the biggest and, according to one source, the 84th largest home in America. Hearst Castle at San Simeon is 12th on the list and remains the largest house in California.

Small tours of Carolands are available, usually two or three times a month. Its popularity has led to a lottery system for tickets. You should submit for than one date to increase your chances of getting on a tour.

Address 565 Remillard Drive, Hillsborough, CA 94010, www.carolands.org, info@calolands.org | Getting there By car only, take I-280 to CA-35. Take exit 36 and then Darrell Road and Ralston Avenue to Remillard Drive. | Hours Check website for tours | Tip Near Hillsborough is Sawyer Camp Trail, a beautiful, six-mile trail located in the San Andreas Fault rift valley (parks.smcgov.org/sawyer-camp-segment).

21_Junipero Serra Statue
The spiritual conquistador of Alta California

The statue is barely noticeable, as it should be, you could argue. You'll find it along Interstate 280, off a northbound exit, overlooking the Hillsborough truck stop, a 26-foot-tall, cement statue of Franciscan friar Junipero Serra (1713–1784). The path up through high grass to the statue includes a sign warning of rattlesnakes. Next to the statue there's a bench on which to sit and contemplate, if nothing else, the roar of traffic streaming below.

The statue suggests a relic out of a studio backlot, a rubble-colored representation of a cartoon character. It was erected in 1976 and it captures Saint Junipero Serra on one knee, pointing west. He seems to be saying something. But what? And why west? Is there a message in the sunset, some hope of redemption in the Pacific Ocean? Or perhaps a warning of some kind? The friar's face looks vaguely menacing.

On the base are carved the names of the missions that Serra helped found.

Friar Serra was born to a poor family in Mallorca, and from a young age displayed a prodigious intellect. At 24, he became a theology professor and was unabashedly ambitious. His dream was to go to the New World, and in 1749 he found himself sailing to Vera Cruz, from where he then walked 200 miles to Mexico City – this despite very poor health. Throughout his life, he built a reputation for his physical toughness and a self-scourging sensibility.

In 1767, with inter-church rivalries raging in Europe, the Spanish Crown called the Jesuits home from the New World. Franciscans took their place and kept up missions in Baja, then gradually expanded into Alta California, to reap economic rewards and to check Russian expansion. Friar Junipero Serra become a dominating administrator and treated the Native Americans brutally. To many, Friar Serra is a symbol of the mission system's oppression. He was declared a saint in 2015 by Pope Francis.

Address Hillsborough Rest Stop, I-280, Hillsborough, CA 94010 | **Getting there** By car, exit at Crystal Springs Safety Roadside Rest Area off CA-280 | **Hours** Unrestricted | **Tip** Nearby is the Crystal Spring Regional Trail with hiking trails surrounding the reservoir. There is street parking along Canada Road (www.parks.smcgov.org/crystal-springs-regional-trail).

22__Johnny's Bar and Grill
Where the Wild Ones still meet

On July 7, 1947, 4,000 motorcyclists roared into the small farming town of Hollister, an hour's drive south of San José. For three days, a 'gypsy tour' of riders with the American Motorcycle Association ran amok. Locals said it was "the worst 40 hours in Hollister history." The seven-man police force was overwhelmed. Fifty people were injured, one hundred were arrested, charged with drunkenness, disturbing the peace, and reckless driving. 'Hot-riding hot heads' told reporters, "We're just having a convention," and drove their bikes into restaurants and bars. The town's main drag, San Benito Street, was littered with broken bottles.

The legend of the 'Hollister riot' was memorialized in a newspaper photo of a man on his cycle waving beer bottles. One journalist said later that the photo was staged and news of havoc exaggerated. Nevertheless, in 1953 Stanley Kramer saw an iconic moment in American cultural history and produced *The Wild One*, the movie starring the incomparable Marlon Brando, and heralded a new film genre: the outlaw biker movie. Hollister, now a town of 40,000, has clung to its historical notoriety ever since and occasionally still sponsors motorcycle rallies, although not every year because event costs are always in dispute.

Ground Zero for the Wild One legacy is Johnny's Bar and Grill, established in 1946 on San Benito Street, where the back of the bartender's T-shirt reads, "Drop your kickstand at Johnny's." One entire wall is devoted to a timeline of town history from the 1930s to the present day, with stills from the Brando film, which was partly shot in Hollister. Johnny's is a sports and biker bar. Patrons are mostly in leather, with key chains dangling, and tattoos are *de rigueur*. On the wall hang local business plaques, bike gas tanks, and memorials, including one to the Boozefighters, the town's original Wild Ones.

Address 526 San Benito Street, Hollister, CA 95023, +1 (831)637-3683, www.johnnysbarandgrill.com | **Getting there** Gilroy Caltrain Hollister to 4th & San Benito | **Hours** Mon–Fri 11–2am, Sat & Sun 9–2am | **Tip** The Northern California Renaissance Faire takes place in Hollister over 12 days annually in early September. Check the website for dates and events (www.norcalrenfaire.com).

23 Ken Kesey's La Honda

On the bus or off the bus?

Highway 84 has switchbacks along the top of the crest of the mountains that run between San Mateo and the coast. Near La Honda, the road loops through dense redwood forests, often draped in thick fog. If you're a Ken Kesey fan, it's easy to imagine the outlines of things that once were. The Merry Pranksters, that group of LSD pioneers and counterculture anti-heroes gathered up by Kesey, had their origins here.

The house Kesey purchased in 1963, flush with cash from his novel *One Flew Over the Cuckoo's Nest*, is about a mile south of Apple Jack's roadhouse. There is a small wooden bridge that crosses La Honda Creek – the house is on the other side, and it's not open to the public. But if you want to wander the roadside imagining the sonic glory that once blasted from giant speakers strung into the redwood trees overhead, no one is going to stop you. It was from this house that the infamous day-glo bus nicknamed 'Further' left on its journey across America in 1964, spreading a swath of psychedelics and anarchy in its wake.

The journey was chronicled by Tom Wolfe in *The Electric Kool-Aid Acid Test*, although the 'Acid Test' had already become famous at the many parties Kesey hosted in La Honda. Allen Ginsberg, Jerry Garcia of the Grateful Dead (see ch. 47), Neal Cassady, Wavy Gravy, Richard Alpert, and various philosophy professors from Stanford all attended. Ironically, Kesey had been a graduate writing student at Stanford in 1960 when he first volunteered to test mind-altering drugs for the US Army. The rest, as they say, is hallucinogenic history.

Apple Jack's, the antique roadhouse / bar in La Honda, was a favorite spot for Kesey and continues to attract an eclectic clientele of locals, bikers, and tourists. First built in 1879 as a blacksmith shop, the shingle-clad cabin is surrounded by redwoods. The back deck has a lovely view of the creek.

Address La Honda, CA 94020, www.lahonda.typepad.com | **Getting there** By car, take CA-84 to exit 24 | **Hours** Unrestricted | **Tip** Take the Heritage Grove Hike to see some of the most spectacular old growth redwoods still standing (www.alltrails.com/trail/us/california/heritage-grove-loop-trail).

24__Hidden Villa

To shelter, inspire, and educate

Many of the gardens and open spaces on the peninsula reflect the progressive visions of California's early settlers, whose entrepreneurial spirit in many ways foreshadowed the tech boom. Much of the land was undeveloped until the 1920s, providing a blank canvas for intellectuals and reformers looking to experiment with new ways of living. One such couple was Frank and Josephine Duveneck, both descendants of prosperous East Coast families – he was the son of the noted painter. In the early 1920s, Frank and Josephine went west and fell in love with the Santa Cruz Mountains. They purchased the land that would become known as Hidden Villa, a living expression of the Duveneck's conviction that the real value of land is its ability to "shelter, inspire and educate."

Frank studied civil engineering at Harvard and was one of the first local landowners to understand the ecological importance of watersheds. He purchased lands adjoining his to keep the watershed intact, a boon to the surrounding ecosystems that still endures. Josephine was dedicated to social justice. Hidden Villa sheltered refugees fleeing the Nazis, Japanese Americans returning from internment camps, and the United Farm Workers looking for a safe place to organize. In 1937, Josephine founded the first traveler's hostel on the West Coast, and in 1945, the first multi-racial summer camp.

Today Hidden Villa is a state-of-the-art sustainable farm and encompasses over 1,600 acres. It's run by a non-profit organization and includes an organic farm, educational gardens, eight miles of hiking trails, and a weekly farmer's market. Generations of Bay Area children have learned about ecology and farming at one of Hidden Villa's many youth programs. It's an excellent place to hike, observe farm animals, and participate in the many special events held year round. The hostel is open from September through May. Pack a basket and have lunch at any of the are several beautiful picnic areas on the grounds.

Address 26870 Moody Road, Los Altos Hills, CA 94022, +1 (650)949-8650, www.hiddenvilla.org, info@hiddenvilla.org | **Getting there** By car, take I-280 to El Monte Road in Los Altos Hills to exit 16. Follow Moody Road to Hidden Villa. | **Hours** Tue–Sun 9am–dusk | **Tip** The local Los Altos History Museum is a very informative museum about the history of the area (51 South San Antonio Road, Los Altos, CA 94022, www.losaltoshistory.org).

25___Page Mill Road
Find Foothills Park

Stanford University is bracketed by two East-West roads: Page Mill Road on the south and Sand Hill Road on the north. The latter, in particular the part that runs through Menlo Park, is the Wall Street of Silicon Valley, the Venture Capital capital that opened in 1972. Sand Hill Road is also home to the Stanford Linear Accelerator Center, otherwise known as the SLAC National Accelerator Lab (see ch. 33).

Page Mill Road runs east to west past the Stanford campus toward the coastal range. Incidentally, just before you reach Highway 280, you'll see the Frenchman's Tower, a 30-foot-tall, red brick battlement behind a wire fence. It has no windows, no doors, and remains an eccentric's folly built in 1875. There are still stories of underground tunnels.

Follow Page Mill Road under the freeway up a curvy, steep, six-mile stretch to the crest. The trek is an ironman's bicycle thrill on the way up and a suicidal run on the way down. At the top, turn left to see Santa Cruz or right to see San Francisco. It's a gorgeous drive in either direction, and there are plenty of trails and overlooks. Visit the open space preserves at Monte Bello and Los Trancos and the Portola Redwoods State Park on the west side of the range, the site of the original Page (saw) mill.

But here's the gem. Halfway up Page Mill road, you come to beautiful Foothills Park. The park is open to Palo Alto residents only, who are required to show proof of residence to a ranger at the entrance kiosk. It is the only park in California with this rule. So take a professor to picnic lunch one afternoon during the week, preferably in winter. The charm is that few people go there, although there's a lake for bass fishing and it is also home to mountain lions and bobcats.

It's just a few miles from the center of Palo Alto to this stunning park with only the sound of an occasional frog. Otherwise, absolute silence!

Address Foothills Park, 11799 Page Mill Road, Los Altos Hills, CA 94022, +1 (650)329-2423, www.cityofpaloalto.org/gov/depts/csd/parks/preserves/foothills/default.asp, open.space@cityofpaloalto.org | **Getting there** By car, take I-280 to exit 20 for Page Mill Road toward Arastradero Road/Palo Alto | **Hours** Daily 8am–dusk | **Tip** Check out the legendary Hewlett Packard Laboratories with their beautiful mosaic decorations on the side walls, which include the original HP rhomboid logo (1501 Page Mill Road, Palo Alto, CA 94304, www8.hp.com/us/en/contact-hp/office-locations.html).

26 Castle Rock State Park

The range out of range

The close juxtaposition of dense urban areas with unspoiled wild landscapes is a defining characteristic of Santa Clara and the Bay Area in general. The rugged forests of the Santa Cruz Mountains, rising like a garden wall between the valley and the coast to the west, have profoundly shaped the outdoor/fitness lifestyle that thrives here. Reserves like Castle Rock State Park, with sweeping views of the coastal ridges, provide the needed antidote to weeks spent inside the confines of a corporate campus. There's no cell phone reception here, which qualifies it in the wired world as a true wilderness – and either heaven or hell for tech types.

Castle Rock is named for the sculpted gray sandstone outcropping that tower on the crest of the ridge. The rock formations, twisted into caverns and ledges, have been a popular spot for bouldering and rock climbing since the sport began. There is usually an onsite outfitter, offering affordable beginning rock climbing lessons, so if you've been waiting to learn, here's the chance. If you'd rather not get roped into anything too adventurous, there are still 34 miles of trails that wind through a swatch of ecosystems and terrains. The trails are linked to an even more extensive system of trails in nearby Big Basin Redwoods State Park.

Many of the area's tallest redwood groves are in the Santa Cruz Mountains, and choosing a route that includes some of these spectacular trees is recommended, particularly in the summer heat. The panoramic views from the area around Castle Rock are among the highest in the range, and on clear days you can see across the ridges to the Pacific. Even here there is a story related to technology. It was thanks to Dr. Russell Varian (1898–1959), a pioneer in the study of x-rays, that the park was preserved. He was also the first scholar to measure the Earth's magnetic field and he used various sites within the park for his calculations.

Address 15000 Skyline Boulevard, Los Gatos, CA 95033, +1 (408)867-2952, www.parks.ca.gov, mtnspecevent@parks.ca.gov | Getting there By car only, take CA-35 to Skyline Boulevard | Hours Daily sunrise–sunset | Tip Next to Castle Rock is Mount Bielawski. The summit is the highest point in Santa Cruz County and sometimes snows in the winter (www.summitpost.org/mount-mcpherson/207752).

27 Holy City

Professor Riker's last communion

Northern California has long been the midnight land of eccentrics and cults. Charles Manson and Jim Jones were perhaps the most ominous and deadly. Add the 'Zebra' murderers, who one might argue were more gang than cult. In sum, there's been a steady stream of con kings. And then there is 'Professor' William E. Riker, who got his 'degree' from reading palms, minds, and perhaps the body language of young women.

He was born in 1873 and lived in San Francisco. When faced with bigamy charges, he fled to Canada, where he opened The Perfect Christian Divine Way. The 'perfect way' doctrine demanded segregation by gender and race. Riker became a notorious white supremacist and ran for governor four times. He was also tried on sedition charges in 1942 because of his support for Adolf Hitler but was acquitted.

In 1918, he bought a 30-acre property along the old Santa Cruz Highway. He later expanded it to 200 acres and built a religious commune known as Holy City. In its heyday, it included 300 people. Among the rules at Holy City was the admonition, "We make it incumbent upon you to report to us at least once a week, either in person or by message. This is to keep you in touch with the vibrations affecting our cult, and for your protection."

To draw interest, Riker placed Santa Claus statues on the side of the road and a billboard that promised, "The Headquarters for the World's Most Perfect Government." When you got there, it was a lively blend of roadside attractions, including a dance hall, peep show machines, a gas station and restaurant, and an alcoholic soda pop bottling plant. In 1940, the old highway was replaced by State Route 17, which guided travelers away from Holy City. Riker converted to Catholicism three years before his death in 1969.

Today, the Holy City, with a few buildings locked up, is considered a ghost town.

Address 21200 Old Santa Cruz Highway, Los Gatos, CA 95033 | Getting there
By car, follow CA-17 S to Madrone Drive, then left on Oneda Court to Holy City Road.
Turn left onto Old Santa Cruz Highway. | Hours Unrestricted | Tip Right off CA-17
is The Cats, a BBQ restaurant with a colorful history from an artist's retreat to a speak-
easy and bordello in the 1920s (17533 Santa Cruz Highway, Los Gatos, CA 95033,
www.thecatslosgatos.com).

28__Auto Vino
Exotic cars and fine wine

Car aficionados would agree that their four-wheeled babies are some of the most beautiful machines on the planet. And it's not just the collectors, mechanics, and drivers who have a love and a lust for cars. The weather in Silicon Valley makes it easy to enjoy classic, luxury, and sports cars. So it only makes sense for someone to create a place where you can pay homage to exotic cars along with a lovely bottle of wine.

In Menlo Park, you will find one such place in Auto Vino, a unique auto showplace and storage space – with wine tastings by Woodside Vineyards. Your experience starts at the back of an unassuming warehouse, where you can see and enjoy rare and exotic luxury cars, sip distinguished wines, smoke cigars, play pool, or even catch the 49ers on a giant TV. You can order a wood-fired pizza or a tri-tip steak sandwich for lunch. Join the wine club to extend the experience.

Auto Vino has become increasingly popular and a go-to setting for corporate soirées for companies such as Facebook, Intuit, Apple, and Google. The venue is also open to individuals hosting private parties.

Within this 20,000-square-foot showroom, you'll find the likes of an S-type Jaguar, a 488 Ferrari, vintage Packards, a DNS Superleggera Aston Martin, a 720S McLaren, and a bevy of Porsches including a 356 and the GT3, as well as a Dodge Demon, the Ferrari FF, a vintage Citroën H Van, and a Bentley GT. The cars are all owned privately and stored here, receiving extraordinary care, including an entry system that manages air flow. Car owners can access their stored cars 24 hours a day, and their cars receive trickle charges and tire rotations. Auto Vino and Woodside Vineyards hold public wine tastings on weekend afternoons. Auto Vino also stores private wine collections in a climate-controlled wine cellar behind the glass wall next to the cars.

Address 205 Constitution Drive, Menlo Park, CA 94025, +1 (650)444-2358, www.autovinogroup.com | **Getting there** Bus 21 to Market Place & Del Norte Avenue, 1.1-mile walk | **Hours** Wine tasting, Sat & Sun 1–4pm; lunch, Tue & Fri 11:30am–1pm | **Tip** Another jewel for car enthusiasts is the more private Candy Store in Burlingame, which is open for tours and special events (1021 Burlingame Avenue, Burlingame, CA 94011, www.candystoreclub.com).

29_Dutch Goose

Where the Stanford Cardinals burger out

In the 1960s, Stanford University decreed that students couldn't drink alcohol within a certain radius from the campus. Consequently, students went further afield to find places like The Dutch Goose, a bar and burger joint in Menlo Park. Half a century later, it remains an innocuous-looking roadside stop with neon beer logos on the outside. Inside, it is a dark warren of a sports bar in early faux-grunge style with peanut shells on the floor, a small pool table, a kids' arcade, an outside bar, benches, booths, and TV screens. Every night is family night. The house favorites include spicy deviled eggs and sweet potato fries. You order your food and drinks at the counter and, if you hear your name called out above the mayhem, you go pick it up.

Iconography at the Goose includes booth backs that were once tabletops, carved to oblivion with initials and notes from patrons, mostly Stanford students. There's a snapshot history of the Western world in sports, business, and statecraft in those carvings. The cardinal, in all its deep scarlet redness, is the mascot for all Stanford sports teams, and the walls are filled with autographed photos of Cardinal sports heroes. The long list of greats includes Tiger Woods, John Elway, John McEnroe, Julie Foudy, Andrew Luck, and Kerri Walsh Jennings, not to mention the coach Bill Walsh. The Stanford sports program has won 23 consecutive Director's Cups, an award given to the most successful Division I sports program in the nation.

The Cardinals' competitive ethos permeates Silicon Valley's start-up culture, which is heavily populated by graduates. Some of the larger companies were themselves started by Stanford grads – Larry Page and Sergey Brin at Google, Jerry Yang and David Filo at Yahoo, Reid Hoffman at LinkedIn, and Evan Spiegel and two frat brothers at Snapchat – who may themselves have eaten at The Dutch Goose.

Address 3567 Alameda de las Pulgas, Menlo Park, CA 94025, +1 (650)854-3245, www.dutchgoose.net | Getting there Bus O, OCA, SE, Y to Tresidder Union | Hours Sun – Tue 11am – midnight, Wed – Sat 11 – 2am | Tip Whether you have kids or not, it's always fun to visit Junior Museum and Zoo, three miles away from The Dutch Goose (1451 Middlefield Road, Palo Alto, CA 94301, www.friendsjmz.org).

30_Facebook Thumbs Up
The hacker's ethos

The street address for Facebook headquarters is 1 Hacker Way, Menlo Park. The place is marked by that iconic graphic, the thumbs up 'Like' sign. It has become a Silicon Valley tourist photo op. Social media fans veer off the highway to bask in the thumb's radiance. There are a few parking spots inside the campus for those who wish to photograph themselves next to the sign. And that's all. There are no tours (nor at any of the other major companies either, although Intel has an informative museum), and the public is not allowed to wander about the campus. Such is the irony: this is, after all, a company that captures user histories and preferences and sells that information to advertisers – and prides itself on a culture of "open communication."

The answer is perhaps in the address itself, 1 Hacker Way, which epitomizes one of the company's prime directives, 'Move fast and break things.' That's both a euphemism for the hacker's ethos and also for the 21st-century notion, and a very personal notion, of 'Live Free or Die.' These slogans and mottos are at the heart of a growing discussion in Silicon Valley about the true price of growth-at-all-costs and, for directors, how to be loyal to both business interests and social values. Put another way: how can you empower users without exploiting them, even endangering them through data breaches?

Facebook, a $300+ billion company, owns Instagram, Messenger, WhatsApp, and Oculus – a virtual reality software and equipment company bought by Mark Zuckerberg for $3 billion in 2014. According to Forbes, Facebook is one of the best companies in the world to work for. The company is looking to grow by another one million square feet in new offices in Sunnyvale. Inevitably, it may also be looking at new coding standards around political advertising and a new understanding with government about the responsibilities of each party.

Address 1 Hacker Way, Menlo Park, CA 94025, +1 (650)543-4800, www.facebook.com |
Getting there Bus D8 to Willow Road & Hamilton Avenue, or Caltrain to California
Avenue | **Hours** Viewable from the outside only from dawn to dusk | **Tip** Just behind the
Facebook headquarters is Bedwell Bayfront Park, where you can enjoy hiking, running,
bicycling, dog walking, bird watching, kite flying, or taking photos (1600 Marsh Road,
Menlo Park, CA 94025, www.menlopark.org/bedwellbayfront).

31 Madera Lounge

Mating habits of the intelligent at the Rosewood

Naturally, it's the matchmakers who really understand life in Silicon Valley. Their stereotypical client is the male venture capitalist or guru-engineer who too often imagines women as exotic algorithms to be 'worked with' and explained on a white chalkboard rather than courted. And so emerges the need for matchmakers to coach and educate, and otherwise serve as a 'love concierge.'

One of the classic date spots in Silicon Valley is the Rosewood Hotel, a California ranch-style hotel, which stands at the western approaches to Silicon Valley, on Sand Hill Road. Sand Hill Road is notable for its concentration of venture capital companies.

It all started when Amy Andersen, Silicon Valley's most popular matchmaker and founder of Linx Dating, hosted her first 'Link and Drink' event at the hotel lounge in 2009. Some have described the Madera Lounge as "the best place to meet your future ex-husband or ex-wife."

The bar is framed in redwood slabs and extends outdoors for a pleasant view of the Coast Range, along with chaises where you can bundle up for a *pas de deux* with a blanket on fresh fall evenings.

Thursday is 'Cougar Night,' which includes a range from ocelots to snow leopards. On the other side, from octopuses to orcas. Conversations sound like this. A single woman on laptop and cellphone: "No, I'm not saying he's not Type A, it's just he's polite and humble." A man to another man: "You don't like the color of the 911? Why don't you get an Aston Martin?"

It's important to note that the bar, regardless of the night, is a longstanding business venue. Nearly everyone seems to be working, networking with other venture capitalists, investors, inventors, or casual meeting with clients if not just seeking company for the night.

The food and cocktails are top notch, and the service is fine tuned. You never know whom you're serving.

Address 2825 Sand Hill Road, Menlo Park, CA 94025, +1 (650)561-1540, www.maderasandhill.com | Getting there By car, take I-280 to Santa Cruz Avenue. Turn left at Sand Hill Road. | Hours Daily 10am–midnight | Tip The Menlo Park Library is supported by volunteers and funds raised through book sales. The bookstore sells books ranging from 50 cents to $2. And don't miss their seasonal book fairs for books ranging from children's lit to antiquarian treasures (800 Alma Street, Menlo Park, CA 94025, www.friendsmpl.org).

32__ Salt Ponds
The salty of the Earth

It's difficult to grasp the size of the salt ponds that line San Francisco Bay from ground level. But if you're flying into SFO, usually coming from the South, get a window seat on the right side of the airplane, and you may see them, littered along the southernmost point of the bay, and then stretching up either side to the Ravenswood salt complex off Menlo Park, and the Eden landing pond complex in Hayward. From above, the ponds look like shards of glass from a broken kaleidoscope, in hues of blue, orange, and magenta; colors depend largely on the kind of microorganisms in a particular pond.

These ponds, which are less than two feet deep, together take up 8,000 acres of bay coastline. In the late 1800s, they were the tech industry of the day and were developed and managed by the Google of the day, Cargill Industries.

Cargill and local environmentalists have had a long relationship over development rights around the ponds to preserve a critical stopover for migratory shorebirds moving through the Pacific Flyway. The low-salinity ponds provide plankton and shrimp for some 70 bird species, including some that are endangered. In recent years, the South Bay Salt Pond Restoration Project, the largest wetland restoration operation on the West Coast, is slowly reintroducing bay water to the ponds and thereby attracting wildlife. Cargill has donated some of its wetlands to the project. Public access to this area is through Menlo Park's Bedwell Bayfront Park.

Salt production begins with bay water pumped into a vast pond system. Complete salinization, from 2.5 percent salt to 25 percent takes four years and ends in crystallizer beds, which are compacted and graded, to allow for mechanical harvesting. The harvested salt is piled up a 90-foot-tall hill in Newark, where it's washed and recrystallized before being shipped to a nearby plant that sells table salt.

Address Bedwell Bayfront Park, 1600 Marsh Road, Menlo Park, CA 94015, www.menlopark.org/Facilities/Facility/Details/Bedwell-Bayfront-Park-6 | **Getting there** By car, take US-101 to Marsh Road in Menlo Park | **Hours** Daily from 7am; see website for seasonal closing times | **Tip** Former Saline City, now a ghost town under the name of Drawbridge, is part of the San Francisco Bay Wildlife Society. You cannot legally visit the area, but you can get a good view from Mallard Slough Trail Spur (www.sfbws.com/drawbridge).

33__SLAC: National Accelerator Laboratory
The heart of quarky science

Driving south from San Francisco on I-280, you can see SLAC cutting through the golden grassland like a runaway storage shed, its impossibly long body reaching far into the distant western horizon. The fact that such a pedestrian-looking structure would be the site of groundbreaking insights into the very nature of matter is part of Silicon Valley's particular mystique.

Built in 1962, the two-mile structure remains one of the longest and straightest in the world. When smashing atomic particles, size really does matter, and soon after the construction of the accelerator, scientists discovered the charmed quark and other basic building blocks of atoms. SLAC also developed the first website in North America.

The accelerator runs underground, while the building above it, known as the Klystron Gallery, houses the equipment that pump energy into the electron beam, as well as laboratory spaces and studios. As the nature of particle physics research has evolved, the uses of the accelerator have also shifted. Much of the work carried out now involves x-ray laser technology using the Linac Coherent Light Source. It's the world's brightest light source, which can record stop-motion movies of chemical reactions and may one day be used to film the processes of living cells.

Free public tours are offered twice a month and are well worth the advanced planning. They offer a close-up look at scientific history in the making. The tour includes the Klystron Gallery as well as the laboratories where scientists from all over the world are at work constructing apparatus for the latest investigations. Scenes on the tour seem lifted off the set of the latest sci-fi adventure movie, where scientists operate complex devices to discover secrets of the universe.

Address 2575 Sand Hill Road, Menlo Park, CA 94025, www.slac.stanford.edu | **Getting there** By car, take I-280 to exit 24 for Sand Hill Road | **Hours** See website for public tours | **Tip** Take a tour at Jasper Ridge Biological Preserve on Sand Hill Road and learn about Earth's natural systems (4001 Sand Hill Road, Woodside, CA 94062, jrbp.stanford.edu/visit).

34 Andy's Orchard

Love among the varietals

A thumbnail history of the greater Santa Clara Valley follows boom and bust cycles threaded through the Ohlone Indian rush, the Spanish colonial rush, the Gold Rush, the oil rush (the valley fed the state most of its oil between 1866 and 1880), and, before the semiconductor rush, a stone fruit rush, which in a limited way continues to this day.

The Santa Clara Valley offers an Edenic blend of well water and an extended growing season, thanks to the protection of the coastal mountains, along with low humidity, the absence of many plant diseases, and the valley's connection to the railroad. Think of Steinbeck's novel, *East of Eden*, pivoting on the novelty of railroads hauling frozen lettuce from Salinas to the East Coast.

From the 1800s on, the 'Valley of Heart's Delight' was covered in orchards. Campbell was nothing but apricots. Sunnyvale was thick with figs, pears, and grain. Grapes grew in Cupertino. Other parts of the valley grew carrots, almonds, walnuts, tomatoes, plums, and cherries. The bounty was accompanied by seed farms, including the Ferry-Morse Seed Company, which opened in 1930 and went on to become the largest flower and vegetable seed producer in the world.

These days, the fruit seed business is centered south of San José in Morgan Hill and includes the Arboreum Company, an Internet business that offers a connoisseur's variety of fruit trees. The company was started by C. Todd Kennedy, who once noted, "Half the named varieties in the national collection come from me." The Arboreum Company is not open to visitors, but nearby is Andy's Orchard, which maintains one of the largest collections of stone fruit varieties on the West Coast, including about 250 varieties of cherries, peaches, nectarines, apricots, and plums. During the summer months Andy Mariani hosts fruit tastings and tours of the orchard. Visitors can sample the fresh, ripe varieties.

Address 1615 Half Road, Morgan Hill, CA 95037, +1 (408)782-7600, www.andysorchard.com, andysorchard@andysorchard.com | **Getting there** Bus 16 to Elm & Half or Half & Mission View | **Hours** See website for seasonal hours | **Tip** For a glass of wine or sparkling champagne, visit family-owned, fourth-generation Guglielmo Winery (1480 East Main Avenue, Morgan Hill, CA 95037, www.guglielmowinery.com).

35_Lick Observatory

Eyes on the sky

Imagine you're in a fictional setting in which you journey up a remote winding mountain road to find a magical wise astronomer. He or she stands in the middle of a polished oak and marble floor, dressed in a long black cloak and peering through the end of a very enormous telescope. Lick Observatory would be that place. It is like a palace of pre-electric scientific inquiry, its white domes rising from Mount Hamilton, 4,000 feet above the Santa Clara Valley.

Before electricity, before electron or radio telescopes, there were simply telescopes made of mirrors and lenses gathering light from the darkened sky. When the 36-inch Great Refractor telescope was built here in 1888, it was the largest in the world. The floor under the telescope was itself an engineering wonder, as it was raised and lowered using wind and water. Built by the University of California, which continues to conduct research here, the observatory was funded by real estate entrepreneur James Lick, whose $700,000 donation (equivalent to over a billion dollars today) was one of the largest in scientific history. In the early 1900s, astronomical photographs perfected at Lick were the first images to reveal the myriad galaxies beyond the Milky Way. The facility is used by more than 100 observers at any given time.

Daytime visitors to Lick Observatory can tour the viewing chambers of both the Great Refractor and the 120-inch reflector telescope in the Shane Dome nearby. There is something of the ancient sciences here, the beautiful floors, the lattice-work of the copper domes, the enormous wheels and cogs that turn the telescopes, the viewing platforms. There are informative exhibits in the main building, not to mention the view from the decks and parking lot. During summer months, there are nighttime programs, including musical performances inside the domes and ongoing amateur astronomy events.

Address 7281 Mount Hamilton Road, Mount Hamilton, CA 95140, +1 (408)274-5061, www.ucolick.org | Getting there By car, follow CA-130/Mount Hamilton Road, turn right on to observatory Peak Road | Hours Thu–Sun noon–5pm | Tip The drive to the observatory passes through Grant County Park, a favorite viewing spot for wildflowers (www.sccgov.org/sites/parks/parkfinder/Pages/JosephDGrant.aspx).

36__Computer History Museum

Shrine to global geekdom

The Computer History Museum in Mountain View is critical in understanding the nature of Silicon Valley as well as the modern era of computer technology. It houses the world's largest collection of computer artifacts and explores the ongoing impact of computing on society today. This is an epic story that incorporates both the history of California and industrial development in America. You don't have to be a geek to appreciate this museum, but if you are one, consider this a pilgrimage.

Housed in a state-of-the-art facility, the museum reflects both the wealth and smarts of the tech world. The multimedia exhibits are arranged chronologically, beginning with the abacus and ending with a Google driverless car. Along the way, visitors can explore the birth of computers, the history of memory storage, programming languages, games, robotics, networking, and the web. All the original equipment and machines are here, set up just as they were when invented or first used. There's also an Enigma Machine from World War II and a recorded interview with one of Alan Turing's co-workers. Turing was the British computer scientist who broke the German communication codes.

Among the museum displays is an IBM 1401 Demo Lab, circa 1959, which lacks only a pencil-skirted secretary to bring it to life. There's an early Apple make-it-yourself computer kit and stations at which to play *Pong* and *Pac-Man*. There's also the Babbage Difference Engine #2, a mechanical, pre-electrical computing engine designed in 1849 by Charles Babbage, who predicted his 'engine' could make mathematical calculations at an unprecedented speed. It was finally built in 1991. This 'steampunk' masterpiece of cogs and levers is run by turning a crank and is demonstrated daily. The exhibits also include recorded audio interviews from the pioneers who brought the digital revolution.

Address 1401 North Shoreline Boulevard, Mountain View, CA 94043, +1 (650)810-1010, www.computerhistory.org | **Getting there** Bus 40 to La Avenida & Shoreline | **Hours** Tue–Sun 10am–5pm | **Tip** Google Android Lawn Statues, a series of foam statues based on the code names for versions of the Android operating system, are just a short walk away (1981 Landings Drive, Mountain View, CA 94043, www.sanjose.org/listings/googleplex-android-statue-garden).

37 Hangar One
The ghosts of Moffett Field

Rear Admiral William 'Billy' Moffett was killed on April 4, 1933. It was a cruel irony for him, because he was regarded as the "father of Naval aviation." Though not a flier himself, no bureaucrat knew the strengths and weaknesses of airplanes better than he did. Moffett was also well-versed in the limits of enormous yet light, helium-filled dirigibles, or air ships. On that April evening, he found himself in the gondola of the USS *Akron*, the first and largest of its kind, a flying aircraft carrier that could launch and retrieve biplanes. Just after midnight, in a bad storm off New Jersey, a series of wind sheers brought the airship down into the freezing Atlantic. Seventy men drowned, including Moffett. Three survived.

Two years later, in 1935, the *Akron's* sister ship, the USS *Macon*, was 20 miles off Point Sur, returning from fleet maneuvers to its home in Hanger 1 at the US Naval Air Station at Sunnyvale, renamed Moffett Field, when once again wind sheers caused structural damage, and felled the *Macon* into the sea. Two died, and the rest of the crew survived. The crash of the two airships scuttled Navy plans for developing flying aircraft carriers. However, the use of blimps continued through World War II.

Moffett Field is a legendary military base. For years, it hosted a P-3C anti-submarine reconnaissance program and the Air Force Satellite Test Center, otherwise known as the Blue Cube. In 1994, Moffett Field was closed and given to NASA's Ames Research Center.

Hangar 1 remains the heart of Moffett. Its footprint covers eight acres, and it's so tall that fog sometimes forms near the ceiling. In 2014, Google signed a 60-year lease from NASA that includes restoring Hangar 1, along with "an educational facility where the public can explore the site's legacy and the role of technology in the history of Silicon Valley." In the meantime, The Moffett Field Museum remains open to the public at Moffett Field.

Address Severyns Avenue, Building 126, Mountain View, CA 94035, +1 (650)964-4024, www.moffettfieldmuseum.org, moffettmuseum@sbcglobal.net | Getting there By car, take US-101 to exit 398. Continue on Moffett Boulevard and take South Akron Road to Severyns Avenue | **Hours** Wed – Sat 10am – 3pm | Tip For Middle Eastern aficionados, try the lamb kebabs at Kabul Afghan Cuisine (351 West Washington Avenue, Sunnyvale, CA 94086, www.kabulrestaurant.net).

38 NASA Ames Research Center

It actually is rocket science

In October 1942, a German V-2 rocket became the first human-made object to reach beyond Earth's grasp, and so began the chronology of the march to the stars. That march is orchestrated in part by NASA, and in particular by the Ames Research Center. It opened in 1939 at Moffett Field as an aircraft research laboratory and gradually evolved into a test facility for NASA's manned space flight program, beginning with Apollo 11. Innovations derived from Ames include everything from the swept-back wing design now standard on most jets, to the blunt body design for spacecraft.

NASA Ames also leads research into Human Systems Integration – in other words, the interaction between humans and complex aerospace systems. A division with 180 people was set up in 1984 with the goal of designing equipment and environments that will enhance human performance during space travel. Related research includes the study of space radiation, lunar dust, and biomedicine.

Current research at Ames is highlighted in exhibits at an elaborate visitor center at Moffett Field. Exhibits include the Marsoweb, a computer program that charts the safest route for Mars Rover landings, and the Reality Theater, where you can see high-resolution images taken from cameras aboard rovers as they cross Martian landscapes studying rocks and soil. Younger children will enjoy the interactive Martian playground, or checking out the Mercury space capsule. SOFIA, the flying observatory that uses infrared technology to record information about distant stars, is also featured. Note the robots being designed for future missions. The exhibits and research suggest a compelling truth, which is that these technologies developed by NASA will most certainly bear real fruit only many decades from now as humanity takes up its search for a new home in earnest.

Address Moffett Boulevard, Mountain View, CA 94043, +1 (650)604-6497, www.nasa.gov/ames/visit | Getting there Bus 81 to Moffett & Middlefield | Hours Mon–Fri 10am–6pm | Tip Charleston Park just north of Moffett Field, next to Google, is a patch of a green space to take a walk or have a picnic here on Earth (1500 Charleston Road, Mountain View, CA 94043).

39__Rengstorff Mansion

Ghosts and all that jazz

The Rengstorff house, the oldest in Mountain View, is a 12-room, two-story, wooden structure built in 1867. It remains a local architectural marvel because of its late Italianate Victorian design. In the 1970s, the home, which originally stood about a mile away from where it is today, was transported to Shoreline Boulevard. It was all but destroyed but was then fully restored in the 1980s and reopened in 1991. It's become a venue for weddings and a well-known preserve for ghost hunters.

Henry Rengstorff was a 21-year-old German man who set out to seek his fortune in America, arriving in San Francisco in 1850 with four dollars. The gold rush was over, so he got a job on a bay steamer sailing back and forth between San Francisco and Alviso. He also worked as a farm laborer, made some money, bought land and then more land, grew grain and fruit trees, acquired cattle, and eventually built a landing that served as a gateway for imports and exports to Mountain View.

Rengstorff died in 1906, and his heirs sold the house in 1959 to a land development company. Over the next 20 years, the property was sold to one owner after another. The local legend is that residents were put off by apparitions. The notion of a haunting gained credibility after interviews with members of the Crump family, the last to occupy the house before it was abandoned, were published. They claimed they heard the sound of a baby crying and someone or something climbing up and down the staircase, and the specter of a 'mournful' woman in an upper window. Moreover, Mr. Crump recounted how he found a hidden stairway leading to a secret room with nothing save a hospital bed and leather restraints.

In the music room, you will see a surprising thing: a framed cover of Dave Brubeck's 1959 jazz album, *Time Out*. Dave Brubeck (1920–2012) was Henry Rengstorff's great-grand-nephew.

Address 3070 North Shoreline Boulevard, Mountain View, CA 94043, +1 (650)903-6073, www.mountainview.gov/depts/cs/shoreline/rengstorff/default.asp | Getting there By car, take US-101 and Amphitheatre Parkway to North Shoreline Boulevard | Hours Tue–Wed 11am–5pm, Sun 1–4pm | Tip Nearby is American Bistro with outdoor seating to enjoy beautiful views of the lake. They'll even pack a lovely picnic basket for you to enjoy outdoors (3160 North Shoreline Boulevard, Mountain View, CA 94043, www.shorelinelake.com/american_bistro.html).

40__ Shockley Semiconductor Lab

The transistor effect

Physicist Dr. William Shockley (1910–1989) was awarded the Nobel Prize in 1956 with John Bardeen and Walter Houser Brattain, "for their researches on semiconductors and their discovery of the transistor effect." Some called theirs one of most important inventions of the 20th century. Shockley is often regarded as the father of Silicon Valley, but of course there are others who could claim paternity. The great Stanford professor Frederick Terman is one. He conceived and developed Stanford Research Park, an early critical mass of tech companies that became part of the Valley bedrock.

And then there are 'the traitorous eight,' who one might think of as stepfathers of the Valley, eight physicists who worked with Shockley in his lab until they couldn't stand him anymore – he was not a benevolent genius. They quit and found a home with Fairchild Semiconductor Corporation, the first high-tech company to work on silicon-based semiconductor devices. Later they formed startups of their own that they developed into companies that have come to define the Valley: Intel, AMD, Microchip Technology, and Kleiner Perkins Caufield & Byers, to name just a few.

The building where the Shockley Semiconductor Laboratory was founded in 1956 is long gone. There is, however, a large statue of a silicon atom and a plaque honoring the lab that reads, *At this location in 1956, Dr. William Shockley started the first silicon device research and manufacturing company in the valley.* Next to the statue is a kiosk with information about the history of the semiconductor industry.

As for Shockley himself, he was a kindly looking man and brilliant, but difficult, mercurial, contradictory. Toward the end of his career he became caught up in eugenics and once proposed that people with an IQ of less than 100 be paid to be voluntarily sterilized.

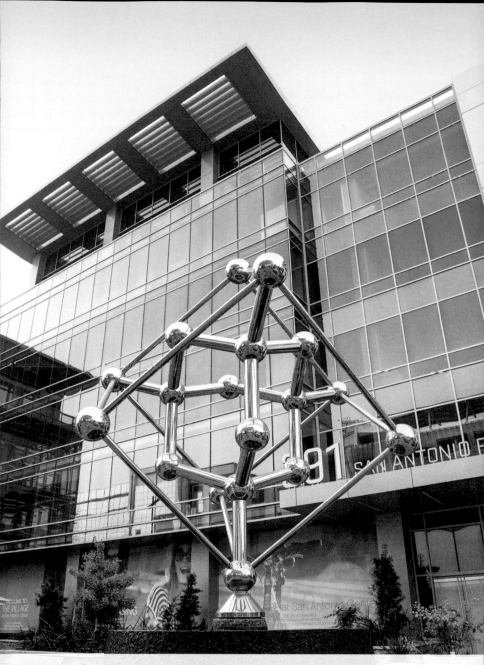

Address 391 South San Antonio Road, Mountain View, CA 94040 | Getting there
Caltrain to San Antonio | Hours Unrestricted | Tip Another iconic place in Mountain
View is Red Rock Coffee, where geeks and hackers gather. There are ample outlets
available, and WiFi is free. Check out their Open mic events or try a coffee tasting
(201 Castro Street, Mountain View, CA 94041, www.redrockcoffee.org).

41 Alta Mesa Memorial Park

Pay homage to Silicon Valley's bright stars

Alta Mesa Memorial Park is a 72-acre, family-owned cemetery, the only nonsectarian one in in the area. Located south of Palo Alto and north of Mountain View, the graveyard opened in 1904. Burial options include three mausoleums, a columbarium, a crematory, and a scattering garden for ashes. A new funeral home was built in 2010, where you can read a memorial book filled with tributes from visitors to those buried there, including Steve Jobs.

Jobs, Apple's co-founder, is known for his tremendous energy, unprecedented innovation, and fierce entrepreneurship. "Have the courage to follow your heart and intuition," he said. He rests in an unmarked grave in this cemetery.

Other patrons include co-founder of Hewlett-Packard David Packard and his wife Lucille with humble headstones side by side and flat on the ground. One of the fathers of Silicon Valley and Nobel Prize-winner William Shockley is there too (see ch. 41), along with screen legend and ambassador Shirley Temple Black, singer Tennessee Ernie Ford, and 49er quarterback Y. A. Tittle.

The gravestones in this leafy cemetery range from traditional and subdued to playful. The epitaph on the headstone of Grateful Dead founder and keyboardist Ron 'Pigpen' McKernan reads, *Pigpen was and is now forever one of the Grateful Dead*. Gus Mozart, the first Volkswagen dealer in California, has a headstone engraved with the image of an iconic VW Beetle.

The gravediggers all have their stories too. One tells of a woman who, fearing oncoming dementia, entered a mausoleum and shot herself. And then there's Larry Wu-Tai Chin, a notorious spy for mainland China between 1952 and 1985. His handlers made him a millionaire, and in order to camouflage his fortune to colleagues at the CIA, Chin adopted the persona of a womanizer and a gambling addict. On the day of his sentencing in 1986, he committed suicide.

DAVID PACKARD
1912 — 1996

LUCILE SALTER PACKARD
1914 — 1987

Address 695 Arastradero Road, Palo Alto, CA 94306, +1 (650)493-104,
www.altamesacemetery.com, rharte@altamesacemetery.com | Getting there Bus 88
to Arastradero & Gunn High School | Hours Daily 7:30am–6pm | Tip Enjoy the
nature and take a hike nearby at Stevens Creek Trail (199 East Camino Real, Mountain
View, CA 94043).

42__Baylands Nature Preserve
Journey to the marshes

The incomparable quality-of-life factor in the Bay Area has always been the seamlessness of urban and rural. From downtown San Francisco, you can be at Muir Woods in half an hour. From Berkeley, you can reach Tilden Park in just a few minutes. In Silicon Valley, the nearness of 'wilderness,' casually defined, is still more striking. The quantity and quality of parks and trailheads is extraordinary, and many are close by. Think of Castle Rock State Park in Los Gatos, to the South; or Purisima Creek Redwoods in the North Valley; or the Sierra Vista Open Space Preserve along the eastern fringes of the valley.

Of course, the situation is changing. There are no more unknown trails, just those less frequented. The truth is, it's becoming a matter of choosing when to go and what limitations you're willing to accept: unleashed dogs, speeding trail bikers, fees, phalanxes of joggers, or the lack of parking.

Here's something to consider: many favorite spots, particularly south of San Mateo, lay along a North-South line east of Highway 280, in the foothills of the Coast Range. There is still less interest to the West in the marshland in East Palo Alto. You can leave Stanford Stadium and follow Embarcadero Road due east, through Palo Alto all the way to the Baylands Nature Preserve. In fact, the road dead-ends at the Baylands Sailing Station. It takes less than 10 minutes. As you enter the Baylands, there's a nature center, open once a week, and a parking area, just at the southern approach to Palo Alto airport, marked by single engine student pilots doing their touch and goes. But it's not a great disturbance. Indeed, the reason to go here, beyond the miles of trails, including access to the San Francisquito Creek Trail, is the silence, the feeling of remoteness, the lavender, the sight of coots and harriers, and the unabashed nature of the marshes.

Address 2500 Embarcadero Road, Palo Alto, CA 94303, +1 (650)617-3156,
www.cityofpaloalto.org/gov/depts/csd/parks/preserves/baylands.asp | Getting there By
car, take US-101 to Embarcadero Road | Hours Daily 8am–sunset | Tip The Abundant
Air Cafe, located next to the airport and the golf course, is a nice lunch place with hot
and cold sandwiches and outdoor seating (1901 Embarcadero Road, Suite 103, Palo Alto,
CA 94303, www.abundantair.com).

43__ The Dish

Waiting for a sign

Set atop a grassy hillside along Interstate 280, the Stanford Radio Telescope, otherwise known as The Dish, is neither the largest nor the most powerful instrument of its kind, yet it's one of the most significant. The Dish, with its 150-foot diameter, was built in 1961 by the Stanford Research Institute at a cost of $4.5 million. It was designed to study atmospheric composition but has also been used to help 'ailing' satellites get back on track when they've lost their orbit. When NASA's *Voyager* spacecraft needed to receive critical information, The Dish was able to get the message through thanks to a unique design in which the radio transmitter and receiver are separate units (a bistatic range radio). That gives The Dish powers other radio telescopes lack. The Dish moves to direct its parabola, depending on the research it supports.

One of the most publicized uses of The Dish has been in the Search for Extraterrestrial Intelligence (SETI). This is the program headquartered in Mountain View, in the SETI Institute, focused on the questions, "What is life, how does it begin, and are we alone?" The plot in nearly every sci-fi movie, from *Close Encounters of the Third Kind* (1977) to *The Space Between Us* (2017), is based on some version of SETI's work. In recent years, scientists at the institute have been discussing whether or not to transmit a message to intelligent extraterrestrials in the cosmos.

The Dish's terrestrial appeal includes some of the most popular hikes in the area. The Dish Loop Trail is a 3.6-mile paved loop that skirts the base of the telescope. The grassy hillside, golden in summer and emerald green in the winter, erupts in springtime in a carpet of blue lupine and California poppies. At its highest point, there is a fantastic view of the surrounding hills and the bay, and on a clear day you can see forever. Or as close as we can hope to come – that is, until someone out there responds to SETI's message.

Address Stanford Avenue & Junipero Serra Boulevard, Palo Alto, CA 94305, dish.stanford.edu |
Getting there Bus SE to Campus @ Mayfield, bus Y to Campus @ Wilbur Field, or bus C to
Bowdoin @ Pine Hill; Stanford bus N Across SV Lot / Lytton Avenue @ Alma Street | **Hours**
See website for seasonal hours | **Tip** The Stanford University Golf Course is located less than a
mile away and has produced many influential professional golfers like Tom Watson and Tiger
Woods. It is open to students, faculty, members and their guests (91 Links Road, Stanford,
CA 94305, www.golfcourse.stanford.edu).

44_El Palo Alto

The Eiffel Tower of Silicon Valley

You'll find it in El Palo Alto Park, a ragged, half-acre swatch of redwood forest between Menlo Park and downtown Palo Alto. An early venue for the Grateful Dead, and a more recent nighttime refuge for the homeless and distraught. Just east of El Camino Real and the railroad tracks. Across from the Stanford Shopping Mall. The park includes a lighted path and a bridge across San Francisquito Creek. And then there it is, just off the path, marked by a bronze plaque – El Palo Alto, 'the tall tree,' a 110-foot-tall *Sequoia sempervirens*, 90 inches in diameter, seven-and-a-half feet in circumference, and a crown spread of 40 feet. And nearly 1,100 years old, according to its rings.

Originally, the tree had three trunks. One is a stump, its fate a mystery. A second trunk got torn away in the flood and winds of 1886. A third remains, but at least 50 feet shorter than it was in the glory days, when they say you could see it all the way from San Francisco. And before that, when Don Gaspar de Portola, the eminent Spanish conqueror, most probably saw it in October, 1769, coming up from the South through what is now San José.

The problem is, El Palo Alto is ill, dying from the top because of parasites, droughts, too many wells, and the particulates in the smoke from passing trains. In the 1920s, many thought the tree wouldn't survive another year. But things have begun to change in the last decade – 'a miracle' – after a sustained campaign to run cleaner trains, cap wells, use air blasts to loosen packed dirt, and uncover young root systems, fix old irrigation pipes, and put in a new PVC pipe that runs to the top of the tree to provide a daily mist.

Among the people who first tried to help save El Palo Alto were Leland and Jane Stanford (see ch. 98), who named their stock farm horse barn in honor of the tree and later used its image in their eponymous university's seal.

Address 117 Palo Alto Avenue, Palo Alto, CA 9430, www.paloaltohistory.org/el-palo-alto.php | Getting there Caltrain to Palo Alto, walk 7-minutes to Palo Alto Avenue and Alma Street | Hours Unrestricted | Tip You'll find a gelato heaven two blocks south at Gelataio (121 Lytton Avenue, Palo Alto, CA 94301, www.gelataio.us).

45_HanaHaus Café

The Bauhaus in workspace

One architectural signature of the digital era is the café/workspace where young programmers and marketeers simultaneously work and caffeinate. They socialize in a freewheeling, sometimes frantic atmosphere. These cafés, which offer proprietary Internet services, customarily include long tables that small groups can book online and use occasionally or daily as an impromptu bricks and mortar workspace. The idea has become particularly popular among young innovators in new startups, as well as investors, 'unicorns,' and aspiring entrepreneurs.

HanaHaus is a classic example of the genre in Palo Alto, which is still the Detroit of the digital era in large measure because Stanford University remains the motherboard of labor, capital, and organizational expertise. The space, along University Avenue, was originally the Varsity Theatre, a single-screen movie 'palace' done in Mission Revival style. Later, it became a Borders Bookstore. When Borders went out of business, the space was transformed and reopened in 2015 as a community office space with a popular courtyard.

The project is a joint venture between HanaHaus and the Oakland-based Blue Bottle Coffee Company. The idea was to incorporate a place where people could gather, share information, and pursue ideas in a café environment. They created a space where the old architectural elements meet new design, including neon colors, glass walls, and minimalistic furniture.

HanaHaus rents out fully equipped conference rooms for small music concerts, NGO board meetings, poetry slams, and lectures. Topics might include 'Quantum Computing for the Curious.'

Breakfast can be delivered to your office. The menu includes waffles with strawberry rhubarb compote. Café 'cocktails' include a siphon bar and New Orleans iced coffee served from a mini-keg. Such is the nature of factory work in the early 21st century.

Address 456 University Avenue, Palo Alto, CA 94301, +1 (650)326-1263, www.hanahaus.com | Getting there Caltrain to Palo Alto | Hours Daily 7am–7pm | Tip The Umami Burger next door offers an ahi tuna burgers and truffle fries, among other exotic bites (452 University Avenue, Palo Alto, CA 94301, www.umamiburger.com/locations/palo-alto).

46 Hewlett-Packard Garage
A legendary tech hatchery

In the history of tech, the creation myth of many great companies begins in a garage. In 1923, Walt and Roy Disney produced their first films in the back of their uncle's house at 4406 Kingswell Avenue in a Los Angeles suburb. In the mid-1970s, Bill Gates and Paul Allen set up shop in the Sand and Sage Motel in Albuquerque. In 1994, Jeff Bezos and his then-wife, novelist MacKenzie Tuttle, created the original Amazon website in a rented garage in a Seattle suburb.

Such is the lore. In 1976, Steve Jobs, Steve Wozniak, and Ron Wayne created Apple in the garage of the 1,800-square-foot home of Mr. and Mrs. Jobs at 2066 Crist Drive in Los Altos. In 1988, Larry Page and Sergey Brin created Google in a garage in Menlo Park, which they rented from a friend, Susan Wojcicki, now the CEO of YouTube. And then there's the garage at 367 Addison Street in Palo Alto, where in 1939 William Hewlett and David Packard manufactured the HP200A audio oscillator. It was a revolutionary device to test sound equipment – among the first customers was Walt Disney, who used eight of the machines in the production of *Fantasia*.

The Hewlett-Packard garage stands in the back of a stately, two-story house on a tree-lined street. The garage, now a private museum, is often referred to as "the birthplace of Silicon Valley."

In recent years, a revisionist history of tech argues that these companies didn't begin in garages, but rather in institutions like Stanford. Page, Brin, Hewlett, and Packard, for example, were all Stanford graduates. Hewlett's MA may be the real source of his creation. An engineering professor, Frederick Terman, in the 1930s pressed students to stay in the area after graduation. Hewlett and Packard took the advice. But while a cluster of institutional support, highly educated labor, and ready capital caused the real big bang, those garages will always have stories to tell.

Address 367 Addison Avenue, Palo Alto, CA 94301, www.hpmuseum.net/divisions,
curator@hpmuseum.net | **Getting there** Bus 35 to Waverly & Homer | **Hours** Viewable
from the outside only | **Tip** To release your shoulders after a week of hunching over your
own computer, enjoy a massage or a soak in a hot tub by booking an appointment at
Watercourse Way Bathhouse Spa, just a five-minute walk from the garage (165 Channing
Avenue, Palo Alto, CA 94301, www.watercourseway.com).

47__Jerry Garcia's Palo Alto
Still following the Dead

The phenomenon that was the Grateful Dead has few parallels in popular music. Combining rock and folk rock songs with long improvised jazz-like riffs, the band led by Jerry Garcia made an art of rambling, freeform concerts designed to get lost in and just enjoy. From the mid-1960s, until Garcia's death in 1995, the Dead, along with the hundreds, sometimes thousands of devoted fans, or Dead Heads, who followed the touring band in caravans across America, were the center of a vast, mobile, countercultural community. Former band members keep the party going with Dead & Company.

Interestingly, the first countercultural community for Jerry Garcia was Palo Alto. It was here in 1961 that Garcia worked as a music teacher at Dana Morgan's Music Store (then at 534 Bryant Street, now a furniture store). In this location, he met Bob Weir and formed a band called the Warlocks. Scores of Palo Alto residents remember guitar or banjo lessons with Garcia. During this period, Jerry perfected his roots/bluegrass-based guitar style, a sound that would profoundly affect the West Coast music of the 1960s.

In 1959, Vernon Gates, a one-time political pollster, opened a coffee house called St. Michael's Alley at 436 University Avenue (now a Peet's Coffee store), which was the only 'coffee house' on the peninsula and attracted a steady clientele of beatniks. Joan Baez sang there, later, Jerry played there too. And yet Gates, ever the businessman, wasn't overly pleased with the clientele. He once said of Joan Baez, then a high school student at Palo Alto High School, "She would go on singing all night and everybody would hang around and not buy anything." And of the Grateful Dead, "The only thing I credit myself with is kicking them out and telling them to go home and practice." A new incarnation of St. Michael's Alley exists now as an upscale brasserie at a new location, a transformation that reflects the cultural history of the town.

Address Peet's Coffee, 436 University Avenue, Palo Alto, CA 94301, +1 (650)325-2091, www.locations.peets.com/ll/US/CA/Palo-Alto/436-University-Ave | Getting there Bus 35 to Hamilton & Waverly, bus C to Lytton Gardens, or Caltrain to Palo Alto | Hours Mon–Fri 5am–8pm, Sat & Sun 6am–8pm | Tip Take in a concert at Shoreline Amphitheatre in Mountain View, which was designed to resemble the Grateful Dead's Steal Your Face logo (1 Amphitheatre Parkway, Mountain View, CA 94043, www.mountainviewamphitheater.com).

48__Pace Art Gallery
From code to à la mode

The best known, arguably most prestigious art galleries remain in San Francisco. A short list might include Modernism, Jack Fischer, Rena Bransten, and Berggruen Gallery. Meanwhile, in Silicon Valley, there are several galleries in San José, notably ZERO1, best known for the ZERO1 Biennial, a showcase of work by international artists and 'technologists' drawn to the intersection of art and technology. Presentations are multi-disciplinary and include visual and performing arts as well as digital media.

And in Palo Alto there's the Pace Gallery, a well-respected contemporary art gallery with locations all around the world, including New York, London, Geneva, Hong Kong, Seoul, Beijing, and Palo Alto. The Palo Alto location perhaps suggests something about the nature of the local art market, not only in terms of wealthy tech buyers from the valley but also the gallery's mission to show the new-new and the most innovative artists. Pace's stable includes Warhol and Mondrian, as well as artists such as James Turrell, Chuck Close, Jim Dine, Claes Oldenburg, and TeamLab, an interdisciplinary group that combine art, technology, design, and the natural world in their art creations. The stable also includes Mainland Chinese acclaimed artists Zhang Xiaogang and Zhang Huan.

The Palo Alto gallery, which opened in 2016, is located on Hamilton Avenue, with its small and unassuming storefront beneath the 1920s Cardinal Hotel. Pace was started in Boston by Arne Glimcher in 1960. His son Marc now runs the business. Mr. Glimcher Sr., who is also a noted film director and producer, has famously recalled that when he started out, there was no actual art business. He bought a Giacometti sculpture in 1964 for a few thousand dollars, *L'Homme qui Marche,* and three years later sold it for $53,000. A similar cast of the sculpture recently sold for more than $100 million at auction.

Address 229 Hamilton Avenue, Palo Alto, CA 94301, +1 (650)561-4076, www.pacegallery.com |
Getting there Caltrain to Palo Alto | **Hours** Tue – Sat 11am – 7pm, Sun 11am – 5pm | **Tip**
Just around the corner is Phyllis, a small clothing boutique where you can buy a fabulous
outfit to attend any museum or a gallery opening in style (540 Ramona Street, Palo Alto,
www.phyllisboutique.com).

49__ The Palo Alto Lawn Bowls Club

Chasing down the pallino

The Sunday afternoon spectacle at the corner of Embarcadero Road and Cowper Street in Palo Alto is life at the Lawn Bowls Club. If you look quickly, you'd think this must be a meeting of hospital orderlies, men and women dressed mostly in white. Striking poses, with a lot of leaning down or resting on one knee, they hurl wooden bowls – not balls because they're asymmetrical rather than perfectly round – the size of softballs, which land with a thud and wander off in some strategic direction. This is followed by much moaning or applause.

Lawn bowling is derived from the 5,000-year-old game that began in Egypt or thereabouts, migrated to Greece and Rome, and 2,000 years later has become the second most popular sport in Europe after soccer. The game was originally played with polished stones, and play began by throwing out a target stone, which became known as a *pallino*, or a 'jack' in lawn bowling.

The game is called *boules* by the French, *bocce* by the Italians, and lawn bowling by the British. The difference between lawn bowling and bocce is that the bocce court is made of sand, or sometimes long grass, and measures 10 feet by 76 feet. The lawn bowling 'rink' is comprised of bent grass, the perfectly coiffed grass that distinguishes British putting greens. Rink dimensions are 19 feet by 120 feet.

At the Palo Alto Lawn Bowl Club, established in 1933, the spirit is both gregarious and evangelical. If you go to observe, there's a good chance a member will approach and talk up the social benefits, tell you about competition with other clubs, including the oldest club in the country in San Francisco, and try to draw you in. The Palo Alto Club has 130 dues-paying members who have access to eight rinks, a clubhouse with kitchen, and locker rooms. The club has become quite popular with tech companies who sponsor team-building events.

Address 474 Embarcadero Road, Palo Alto, CA 94301, +1 (650)323-2575, www.palbc.org | Getting there Bus 22 El Camino & Sam McDonald, or bus E, Tech Line to Palo Alto High School | Hours See website for schedule | Tip Next door to the club is the Elizabeth F. Gamble Garden, a magic place where you can relax and enjoy beautiful flowers (1431 Waverley Street, Palo Alto, CA 94301, www.gamblegarden.org/visit-us/plan-your-visit).

50___ The Palo Alto Post Office

The city that Birge built

Palo Alto is a city of 67,000 people just across the Camino Real from Stanford University. The town was founded in the 1850s and is widely regarded as the birthplace of Silicon Valley, in part because of the famous collaboration of Dave Packard and Bill Hewlett that began in the 1930s in a one-car garage at 367 Addison Avenue (see ch. 46).

The city has always been an architectural showcase. You'll find distinctive structures like Hanna House designed by Frank Lloyd Wright (see ch. 100), or MacArthur Park designed by Julia Morgan, hundreds of homes designed by Joseph Eichler (see ch. 83), and homes by William Wurster and Joseph Esherick.

But a single architect named Birge Clark (1893–1989) designed most of the buildings in town, more than 450, built from the 1920s through the 1960s. Palo Alto has been called 'The City that Birge Built.' As Palo Alto historian Steve Staiger once said referring to Clark, "He's our Maybeck, he's our Julia Morgan."

Clark designed the Norris House, most of the 500 blocks of Ramona Street, a Spanish-style historic district, the Hewlett-Packard plant, and the Hoover family home at 623 Mirada Road, where Herbert Hoover received news of his election as the US president in 1928.

Clark also designed the unique local post office at 380 Hamilton Avenue.

In the 1920s, most post offices were designed in a Beaux-Arts style, but Clark chose Mediterranean Revival, which had enormous local appeal, hence so much of the architectural style at Stanford. The post office features a tile roof, an open arcade with round arched entryways at both ends, and an ornate lobby. There has long been a debate over whether Clark was more interested in form or function. Those closest to him claim he was more interested in how a building worked than how it looked, but we have the good fortune to be able to enjoy both aspects of his work.

Address 380 Hamilton Avenue, Palo Alto, CA 94301, +1 (650)321-1423, www.pastheritage.org/ Articles/PostOffice.html | Getting there Caltrain to Palo Alto | Hours Unrestricted from the outside, Mon–Fri 8:30am–5pm, Sat 9am–3pm | Tip Right around the corner is Coupa Café where you can treat yourself to organic single-estate coffee and sweet snacks. The café supports local, organic, sustainable, and family-run farms (538 Ramona Street, Palo Alto, CA 94301, www.coupacafe.com).

51_Palo Alto Public Art Tour

The street as gallery

From a grove of blue trees to a school crosswalk painted to look like a stream full of koi, to outdoor tables sheltered by giant metal California poppies, the artworks of Palo Alto's Public Art Program bring a sense of city as art gallery. The collection includes more than 100 permanently installed pieces of art, and almost 200 temporary or portable pieces. Any walk through the city's public parks or buildings is apt to reveal an artwork, though obtaining the online map and guide to the collection is the best way to see the full range of works.

Each public art piece is specifically chosen to interact with the neighborhood in which it is installed. Many of the artists are local and inspired by Palo Alto in their work, so an interplay between art and place is continually present. For example, the granite sculpture *Arpeggio V* at the Mitchell Park Library and Community Center, uses book-shaped blocks of granite to create a sort of archway. Other works, such as Fletcher Benton's *Tilted Donut #5*, a massive abstract corten steel sculpture, seems to echo the speed of heavy traffic on the corner of El Camino Real and Page Mill Road. The recent installation *Foraging Islands*, built along the Bay Shore, is an environmental sculpture made from city tree trimmings and woven into a small island that creates foraging space for shore animals. The process of its construction by volunteers was part of the work conceptually.

One agenda in the public art program is to reveal the creative work that takes place behind so many office doors in Palo Alto. This initiative known as Code:ART encourages electrical engineers, coders, and techies of all stripes to collaborate in public art making. Past installations included *The Murmur Wall*, by Future Cities Lab, a light sculpture using LED light streams and text displays to convert real-time data streams into light patterns.

Address Multiple locations, Palo Alto, CA, www.cityofpaloalto.org/gov/depts/csd/public_art/default.asp | Getting there See website for locations | Hours Unrestricted | Tip The City of Palo Alto and the National Endowment for the Arts held the Code:ART Festival in 2017 to turn the city into a "laboratory for urban interventions and creative placemaking." Look for some of the works of art around town (www.cityofpaloalto.org/gov/depts/csd/public_art/codeart.asp).

52 Roth Building
The birthplace of group medicine

For those interested in urban archeology, there's no better example of a town's identity revealed through a building's history than at 300 Homer Avenue in Palo Alto. This is the Roth Building, once known as the Palo Alto Medical Clinic. The two-story Spanish Eclectic-style building, with red clay tile roof and a courtyard anchored by a large valley oak, was designed by architect Birge Clark. The building has become famous for the warm-toned frescoes that line the front. It now languishes in disrepair but awaits transformation into a local museum.

The building was constructed in 1932 to serve as a clinic for a group of doctors who banded together in a shared practice. The group was led by Dr. Russell Lee, and his partnership became the first medical group practice in the country and was harshly condemned at the time as being suspiciously socialist.

In San Francisco, during the same period, another socialist, the Mexican artist Diego Rivera, was working on murals at the San Francisco Art Institute. He worked with an assistant named Victor Arnautoff (1896–1979), a Russian émigré. Arnautoff drew Dr. Lee's attention and was chosen to create frescoes for the new clinic. He chose subjects that included notable physicians and illustrated modern medical breakthroughs, contrasted with older notions of medical practice. There are four painted medallions depicting Lister, Hippocrates, Pasteur, and Roentgen. To the left of the main entrance is Dr. Emmett Holt (1855–1924), an important pioneer in pediatric medicine. To the right of the main entrance is an image of an influential Canadian physician / teacher, Sir William Osler (1849–1919), shown examining a woman with bare breasts. The image of the half-naked woman drew outrage in the community, along with constant traffic jams. The monochrome image underneath it shows a witch doctor performing an exorcism.

Address 300 Homer Avenue, Palo Alto, CA 94301 | Getting there Caltrain to Palo Alto, 11-minute walk | Hours Viewable from the outside only | Tip The nearby Museum of American Heritage is a small, local museum highlighting games, toys, and gadgets that shaped American Culture (351 Homer Avenue, Palo Alto, CA 94301, www.moah.org).

53__Stanford Powwow
Snake Dance like the ancestors did

California's blue-state, blue-sky image is tinted by a dark history of racial oppression. Treatment of the Chinese and Japanese come to mind, along with Hispanics. But often forgotten are the indigenous peoples. The figures are not agreed upon, but by one estimate there were at least 300,000 Native Americans in California when the Spanish arrived in force in the 1760s. By 1900, the number had fallen to less than 25,000. The Gold Rush period between 1850 and 1875 was particularly pernicious.

The Native American population in the state is now around 700,000, the largest in the United States. And indigenous culture continues to flourish. Nowhere do you see a more vibrant expression of that culture than at the annual Stanford Powwow. Sponsored by the Stanford University Native American Cultural Center, the Powwow is one of several exciting events centered on Native cultures, including the annual Stanford Hawai'i Club Lu'au, a celebration of Native American Heritage month, plus monthly community dinners. For Indigenous Peoples' Day in October, the students attend a vigil on campus and the Bay Area Indigenous Peoples' Day Sunrise Gathering on Alcatraz.

The Powwow is not to be missed. One of the biggest in the state, the three-day, student-run festival takes place every May, set in a eucalyptus grove on the Stanford University campus. It began in 1971 and draws thousands of Indians from tribes across the country. Those often represented include the Dine, Miwok, Northern Arapaho, Cheyenne River Sioux, Umatilla, Tlingit, Blackfeet, Jicarilla Apache, Shoshone-Paiute, and Santa Clara Pueblo. Festival highlights include drumming, singing, and competitive dancing such as Snake Dance and Shawl Dance. Well-known dancers include Trae Little Sky and the illustrious Head Woman dancer Jocy Bird. Shop for handmade wares and enjoy Native American flavors too.

Address Eucalyptus Grove, Galvez Street & Campus Drive East, Palo Alto, CA 94305, +1 (650)723-4078, powwow.stanford.edu, powwow-cochairs@lists.stanford.edu | **Getting there** From Palo Alto station, take bus SE to Tresidder Union (Lagunita Drive East) | **Hours** Annually on Mother's Day Weekend in May, Fri–Sun | **Tip** Also on Stanford's campus is Muwekma-Tah-Ruk, the Native American House. The name means 'House of the People' and student residents volunteer at the lu'au and the powwow. You can go see it, but it is not open to the public (543 Lasuen Mall, Stanford, CA 94305, www.resed.stanford.edu/residences/find-house/muwekma-tah-ruk).

54__The Stanford Theatre
Restoring Hollywood's golden age

Among the notable old movie palaces in the Bay Area, you think of the Rialto in Sebastopol, the Castro in San Francisco, and the Stanford Theatre in Palo Alto, on University Avenue. The theater's niche is the golden age of cinema, between 1920 and 1965. It's the perfect portal to appreciate the founders of Hollywood, such as cinematographer Arthur Edeson, director Alfred Hitchcock, and, of course, Garbo, Kelly, and Cooper – and many others.

The Stanford Theatre was built in 1925 for $300,000 and originally had 1,454 seats, now reduced to 1,175. The theater was exquisitely restored in the late 1980s by the David and Lucile Packard Foundation, which bought it for nearly $8 million and put in another $6 million. The restoration holds closely to the Greek-Assyrian style expressed by the original architects, Weeks and Day. They were top in their profession in the 1920s and designed some of San Francisco's great hotels, including the Huntington, the Mark Hopkins, and the Sir Francis Drake Hotel.

Charles Peter Weeks (1870–1928), with a small mustache over a tight mouth, was a 'design moralist' and a blasting critic of San Francisco's turn-of-the-century architectural practices, which he derided and believed increased the devastation caused by the 1906 earthquake. Weeks married a member of New York's *beau monde*, Beatrice Woodruff, on the day after her divorce from an attorney whom she accused of cruelty, including the time he kissed her on a public street. Five years later, Weeks died from a heart attack. Later, Beatrice married the great horror actor Bela Lugosi, but the marriage lasted only a year.

Before and after the 7:30pm show, local organ masters still perform on the theater's Mighty Wurlitzer. Among them, David Hegarty, best known for his long association with the Castro Theater, and for his film music transcriptions from Hollywood's golden age.

Address 221 University Avenue, Palo Alto, CA 94301, +1 (650)324-3700, www.stanfordtheatre.org | **Getting there** Caltrain to Palo Alto | **Hours** See website for schedule | **Tip** Next door is a spacious lunch and dinner spot, Local Union 271, where the tomato soup comes highly recommended (271 University Avenue, Palo Alto, CA 94301, www.localunion271.com).

55 _ TEDx Palo Alto

Welcome to the brain spa

A key aspect of Silicon Valley culture is the evangelization of new ideas: hence TEDx, the online speaker's conference that has made celebrities out of scientists, entrepreneurs, academics, and experts in every field, no matter how arcane. The grail is to spread great ideas, challenge cultural assumptions, and equally important, stimulate creativity and inspiration. And do it in 20 minutes.

These conferences have become a nonprofit industry of their own, and their bricks and mortar address is no longer important. Popular sites, each with their own take, include 99U, Ignite, Big Think, PechaKucha Nights, the Veritas Forum, and the Moth, which is tuned more to storytelling than lectures.

The mother of speaker events is TED, whose conferences debuted in 1984 in Monterey, an hour south of the valley. The TED acronym stands for "Technology, Entertainment, Design," and was created by Richard Wurman, an architect and graphic designer, and Harry Marx, sometimes referred to as the father of modern broadcast design. In 2001, TED was bought by Chris Anderson, whose interest in 'radical openness' lead to the TEDx initiative in 2009, whereby local organizers anywhere in the world can obtain free licenses to sponsor their own TED talks.

The list of speakers includes scientists, philosophers, artists, actors, musicians, business and religious leaders, philanthropists, writers, and many others. Among many TED presenters are Marina Abramovic, Jimmy Carter, Frank Gehry, Naomi Klein, and Dr. Jane Goodall.

With planning, visitors to Silicon Valley can attend these smaller TEDx talks. They're often held in high schools around Silicon Valley, as well as at the TEDx Palo Alto Salon. Ticket prices are less than $100. As for the 'main' five-day, annual TED talk conference, it's held in different cities along the West Coast. You must become a Conference Standard Member to attend.

Address TEDx Palo Alto, Schultz Cultural Arts Hall at the Oshman Family JCC, 3921 Fabian Way, Palo Alto, CA 94303, www.tedxpaloalto.com, info@tedxpaloalto.com | Getting there Bus 88, 824 to Fabian & Charleston | Hours See website for schedule | Tip Close by is the Golden State Youth Orchestra for music education and excellence, where you can attend a concert (4055 Fabian Way, Palo Alto, CA 94303, www.gsyomusic.org).

56 Duarte's Tavern
An old-fashioned chat room

Pescadero's first heyday was in the 1920s, but then at the end of the decade the town was nearly burned down. In the 1960s, the town acquired a reputation as a lunch break between Half Moon Bay and Santa Cruz, a black-and-white photo of a town, two miles off Route 1, where you could buy a postcard or fresh vegetables, and cool your palms with a beer or a stinger at Duarte's Tavern.

Duarte's survived the fire and has been the town's mainstay watering hole since 1894, when people stepped out of their buggies for a fountain lunch and Spreckle's ice cream. The Portuguese family that started it still owns it four generations later, and the chefs and waiters are still mostly people who live within walking distance of the restaurant. Duarte's motto remains, 'Simple dishes, nothing fancy.'

Ron, the latest patriarch, died in 2017. For decades, he and his wife Lynn lived upstairs just above the restaurant's jukebox. Ron was obsessed with his gardens. Every morning he went off to Half Moon Bay to buy fresh fish, and then he'd scour his gardens behind the restaurant, looking for the best artichokes, leeks, and lettuce, as well as olallieberries, 'the king of blackberries.' Their olallieberry pie is as famous as their artichoke soup and crab *cioppino*.

In the last decade, Pescadero, with a population of less than 700, has enjoyed a second heyday. It's an overnight romantic getaway, just over the mountains from Palo Alto, and a lovely place to browse for furniture, local wines, fresh bread, and goat cheese – note the Harley Farms Goat Dairy. It's also become part of the renaissance of small organic farms now proliferating in this part of the coast, under the banner of 'Food Justice.' Pie Ranch is one such farm to visit. Also spend an afternoon at Año Nuevo State Park, where you can join tours to see wildlife in the area, including lounging elephant seals.

Address 202 Stage Road, Pescadero, CA 94060, +1 (650)879-0464, www.duartestavern.com |
Getting there Bus 17 to Stage Road & Pescadero Creek Road | Hours Wed–Mon
7am–10pm | Tip For delicious, freshly baked artichoke garlic bread, stop at the Arcangeli
Grocery / Norm's Market, just down the street from Duarte's. Behind the grocery, next to
Pescadero Creek, is a park with picnic tables (287 Stage Road, Pescadero, CA 94060,
www.normsmarket.com).

57__Bair Island

Birders' paradise

Bair Island is a 3,000-acre tidal marsh just south of Redwood Shores, which is home to EA (Electronic Arts) and Oracle, among others. The island has never been developed, although over the decades it was occasionally used by farmers and cow herders, and then, in the mid-20th century, by salt producers. Today, Bair Island (which is actually three islands) is all but invisible, although as you drive along Highway 101, you may catch the scent of salt and the sight of pickleweed or waving yellow gumplant, depending on the tide.

The islands are home to all kinds of grasses, ox-tongue, and thistles, along with young Chinook salmon. Harbor seals come to breed, and shorebirds abound, including plovers, shovelers, avocets, goldfinches, burrowing owls, and black-necked stilts. Among the population there are several endangered species, including steelhead, the salt marsh harvest mouse, double-crested cormorants, the salt marsh wandering shrew, and Ridgway's rail, formerly the California clapper rail, which is the size of a chicken and doesn't often get off the ground.

Bair Island, part of the Don Edwards San Francisco Bay Area National Wildlife Refuge, has been the site of a series of skirmishes between ecologists and developers. Housing developments on the marshland have been approved and shut down over the years. Scientists believe the bay needs 100,000 acres of healthy marshland to maintain ecological harmony, and Bair Island's 3,000 acres is a significant part of that area.

The island offers several hikes, facilitated by a bridge that connects the trails. Tour guides are available to show the glories of the island, which include sightings in the sloughs of large rays and small leopard sharks along the outer edges. The place to start is in Redwood City off Whipple Avenue on Bair Island Road, where the path winds around and comes to a trailhead, which leads to a 1.7-mile, very easy hike. Bring binoculars.

Address Bair Island, Whipple Avenue and East Bayshore Road, Redwood City, CA 94062, www.wildlife.ca.gov/Lands/Places-to-Visit/Bair-Island-ER | Getting there ECR bus to El Camino Real & Whipple Avenue, 15-minute walk east | Hours Daily dawn–dusk | Tip After a hike, grab a drink and tasty scotch eggs nearby at Martins West Gastropub (831 Main Street, Redwood City, CA 94063).

58_Oracle Headquarters
Tales of a Samurai sailor

Above Redwood City, just east of Highway 101 and along the Marine Parkway between a slough and a lagoon, you will see the campus of Oracle, makers of "the most important software nobody's ever heard of." This is Oracle's headquarters, once known as the Emerald City, and also Larryland. It was designed by KSH Architects, whose other clients include Stanford University and prestigious clubs like the Bohemian Club and the Menlo Circus Club (see ch. 2). The Oracle campus includes 12 buildings with offices for 12,000 employees. From one angle the buildings all look like huge stacks of poker chips. And you can schedule a tour of the place simply by calling an Oracle sales representative and seeing about making arrangements far enough in advance.

The Oracle campus features a university, the public Design Tech High School, and a pond decorated with a 90-foot, wing-powered trimaran, known as *USA 17*. This was the boat – and a true product of rocket science – that won the 2010 America's Cup. This three-hulled sloop could sail upwind or downwind faster than the true wind that powered it. Such was the dream of Larry Ellison, Oracle founder, and CEO until 2014, the $61-billion man, the consummate salesman with an attraction to first place, fast bikes, foiling boats, lengthy motor yachts, and exotic car collecting. And then there was his 8,000-square-foot replica of a Japanese palace, set on 1.7 acres in Atherton.

Ellison, now 75, is reminiscent of an early 20th-century tycoon, the flamboyant, controversial, persona who loves *The Art of War*, admires Samurai doctrine, and holds the conviction, "If you want to compete with me, prepare to be crushed." Critics on the Internet write about Oracle's culture being "driven by fear." Yet, he's also been a steady philanthropist, unlike other local innovators who are not known for their generosity, at least publicly.

Address 500 Oracle Parkway, Redwood City, CA 94063, www.oracle.com/corporate/contact | **Getting there** Bus 60, 67, 260 to Marine Parkway & Twin Dolphin Drive | **Hours** Contact Oracle to schedule a tour. Pond and *USA 17*, dawn–dusk | **Tip** If you would like to walk by three of Silicon Valley's largest tech companies, walk along the Bay Trail, which takes you by the Oracle, Facebook, and Google headquarters (www.rhorii.com/RedwoodShores/RedwoodShores.html).

59__Pulgas Water Temple

A monument to the real Gold Rush

It's an old and often a blithely ignored truth that California's fate is tied to water. Roman Polanski's 1974 film noir, *Chinatown*, is always brought up as the artistic representation of the problem. Marc Reisner's 1986 book, *Cadillac Desert*, is the definitive nonfiction book on the subject. The American West, Reisner famously wrote, is a vast emptiness "amid a civilization whose success was achieved on the pretension that natural obstacles do not exist."

Since the 1850s, 'water wars' in California have pitched North against South, farmers against city dwellers, and big corporations against environmentalists. In much of the last decade, the situation has worsened because of drought. The core debate pits the needs of urban and agricultural users against conservationists trying to preserve the integrity of water sources.

Much of Silicon Valley gets its drinking water from local reservoirs and groundwater, but mostly from the Sierra Nevada – notably from the Hetch Hetchy reservoir in Yosemite National Park. High mountain water runs down the Tuolumne River and then through 160 miles of pipes to the Upper Crystal Spring reservoir in San Mateo County. The system took 24 years to build and is honored at the Pulgas Water Temple.

The temple, with its Beaux-Arts style, was designed by William Merchant, a student of Bernard Maybeck. When the temple opened in 1934, it was considered a godsend by San Francisco, which was unable to withstand the fires after the 1906 earthquake, being solely dependent on groundwater. The temple, with its reflecting pools, is reminiscent of a Maxfield Parrish painting, something grand and, in a certain light, deeply sentimental. It's built on the landing site of the Spanish Portola Expedition, which arrived in 1769. The area became part of a land grant named Rancho de Las Pulgas, or Ranch of the Fleas.

Address 56 Cañada Road, Redwood City, CA 9406, +1 (650)872-5900, www.sfwater.org | **Getting there** By car, follow I-280 N to Edgewood Road in San Mateo County. Take exit 29 and follow Cañada Road. | **Hours** Mon – Fri 9am – 4pm | **Tip** The Peninsula Museum of Art in Burlingame has a large stable of California artists, some of them with studios in the building. Check the museum's website for classes and events (1777 California Drive, Burlingame, CA 94010, www.peninsulamuseum.org).

60___Resolution Trail
Among the legacies of Flight 304

William Kapell was a child prodigy who won his first music competition at 10. In his 20s, he became famous for his interpretation of Aram Khachaturian's *Piano Concerto in D-Flat.* Alistair Cooke, in his series *Letter from America,* wrote about Kapell, "He was a small man with black hair and black eyes, eyes at once fierce and melancholy. An amiable, impulsive, gentle man, except when he sat down at a keyboard."

Kapell was obsessive about practicing and always took his concert grand piano on tour, including to Australia where in 1953 he gave 37 concerts. The last was in Geelong and included a performance of Chopin's *Funeral March Sonata.* Kapell began his trip back to America a few days later, promising never to return after some unusually tough reviews.

He caught British Commonwealth Pacific Airlines Flight 304, a Douglas DC-6 named *Resolution,* which left Sydney on October 28. Coming to final approach to SFO, seven miles southeast of Half Moon Bay, at 8:43 in the morning of the 29th, in heavy fog, the plane crashed. Nineteen passengers and crew were killed. Investigators concluded the probable cause was pilot error. The site has been memorialized with a rock monument and a trail in El Corte de Madera Creek in Open Space Preserve.

The preserve is off Skyline Boulevard, nine miles south of Highway 92, starting at Skeggs Point. Resolution Trail is 6.2 miles and absolutely gorgeous, shaded with majestic redwoods, Douglas fir, and manzanitas. It turns to the drier, rockier landscape near the steep top. The trail is also well known for large sandstone monoliths called tafoni, rock formations with beautiful natural and fragile cavities dotted throughout.

As you walk along the trail, you may discover bits of debris, which you are asked not to take away. The site is surrounded with the redwoods and silence, which is perhaps a good place to reflect on life.

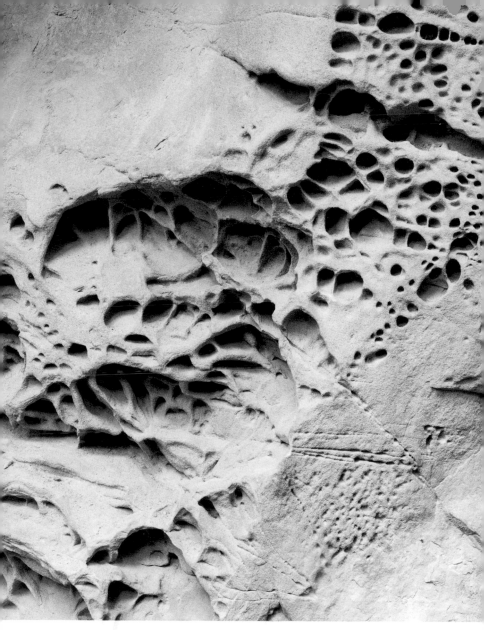

Address Skyline Boulevard, Redwood City, CA 94062, www.openspace.org/preserves/
el-corte-de-madera-creek | Getting there By car, take CA-35 to Skeggs Point. From
parking lot, walk north along Skyline Boulevard and enter through gate CM01. Take El
Corte de Madera Creek Trail, then North Leaf, Methuselah, and Fir Trails. Turn left onto
Resolution Trail. | Hours Daily dawn–dusk | Tip Stop at Roberts Market for a hearty
sandwich before or after your hike (3015 Woodside Road, Woodside, CA 94062,
www.robertsmarket.com).

61_San Carlos Airport
Flight times to Burning Man

Organizers are always emphatic that Burning Man is not a festival but rather an "experiment in community and art." Whatever it is, it lasts a week at the end of every August and has become a magnet for Silicon Valley's founder class, as well as 'founder hounders.' The Burning Man site is 100 miles northeast of Reno, Nevada. So one way that people get there from Silicon Valley is to thumb a ride on executive jets taking off from San Carlos Airport. The airport, a mile south of Oracle headquarters, is home to 500 airplanes and serves as a 'reliever' airport for San Francisco International Airport. It's one of eight small strips around the Bay Area with a control tower.

San Carlos Airport, with its single 2,600-foot runway, runs parallel to Highway 101, at the Holly Street exit, and includes the Hiller Aviation Museum, which is well worth a visit on its own. More than 40 aircraft are on display, including planes, experimental models, helicopters, and gliders, some of which are replicas. The collection has examples from nearly every decade since 1869 when Frederick Marriott conceived of a steam-powered airship that would fly gold rushers from New York to San Francisco. The museum features a full-motion flight simulator, the kind usually found only at flight schools; an Invention Lab with a hands-on approach to design, engineering and aerodynamics; and a nano drone workshop with a flight simulator.

The airport also includes a popular local eating spot, a diner known as the Sky Kitchen. It's just across the runway from the museum and specializes in a killer breakfast burrito with hash browns or diced ham and scrambled egg with hash browns. Open 6am to 3pm seven days a week, the Sky Kitchen is a hangout for pilots and techies as well as for those who enjoy sitting in a booth or at the counter and watching small planes come and go.

Address 601 Skyway Road, San Carlos, CA 94070, +1 (650)573-3700, publicworks.smcgov.org/san-carlos-airport | **Getting there** By car, take US-101 to exit 411 toward Redwood Shores Parkway. Take Skyway Road. | **Hours** Daily 10am–5pm | **Tip** The Bay Trail through Redwood Shores leads over a wide variety of surfaces, from paved bike paths to gravel and dirt paths. You can hike it as a loop trip around the Redwood Shores peninsula (www.rhorii.com/RedwoodShores/RedwoodShores.html).

62 Alviso

A little-known refuge for the curious

The southernmost end of San Francisco Bay is a desolate yet beguiling landscape noted for creeks, sloughs, and salt ponds. Among the signs of life here is Drawbridge, which was officially designated a ghost town in 1979 on Station Island, several miles south of downtown Fremont. The town consists of a handful of buildings not open to the public. From the air, the place looks like dice thrown down on velvet marshland.

The presiding ruin is a railway station next to the remains of a narrow-gauge railway, all of which are now sinking into the bay. During its heyday in the mid-1870s, a sole operator raised and lowered two drawbridges 10 times a day. When his workday was done, he returned to his cabin, his whiskey, and a few friends.

A mile-and-a-half to the southwest of Drawbridge, between Sunnyvale and Milpitas, you'll find the neighborhood of Alviso, a 900-acre dot on the map, 13 feet below sea level, population 2,128, now a San José suburb. It is named after Juan Ignacio Alviso (1772–1848), a soldier in a Spanish expedition, who settled down in Santa Clara County and was awarded a large land grant, known as Rancho Rincón de Los Esteros, which could be translated as Estuaries Bend.

A century-and-a-half later, Alviso has the atmosphere of a studio backlot that would be best suited for the film noir genre. In fact, it was a Mexican fishing village at one time. You'll note some of the old, wooden fishing sheds, now fallen over in piles and ruins. Along with palm trees and a steady breeze, Alviso has a bait shop and a mobile home park. But the religious centers, including Our Lady Star of the Sea Roman Catholic Church, the Balaji Buddhist Temple, an Islamic Center, and the Taiwanese American Center represent a diverse community. Several Mexican restaurants serve hikers visiting Marina County Park, and, in their team T-shirts, from Google and Facebook.

Address Alviso, San José, CA 95002, www.sanjose.org/neighborhoods/alviso | **Getting there** Bus 58 along North 1st Street | **Hours** Unrestricted | **Tip** Alviso Marina County Park, the bayside park in Alviso, is a beautiful spot for hiking, biking, and bird watching (1195 Hope Street, San José, CA 95002, www.sccgov.org/sites/parks/parkfinder/Pages/AlvisoMarina.aspx).

63 Avaya Stadium

Eat, drink, pray, win

There are three professional sports teams in Silicon Valley, all take their names from the major cities at both ends of the valley. And so the San Francisco 49ers, a National Football League team, whose home is in Levi Stadium in Santa Clara, the San José Sharks, a National Hockey League team that plays at 'the shark tank' in downtown San José, and The San José Earthquakes, a Major League Soccer team based near the San José airport.

The Earthquakes, founded in 1994, play in Avaya Stadium, named after the $3.2-billion maker of Internet telephony systems. The company, which went in and out of Chapter 11 in 2017, created the first 'cloud-enabled' stadium, offering what were then revolutionary features: Wi-Fi, a real-time fan app, and a digitized 'fan engagement wall,' with multimedia content and aggregated social media feeds.

The stadium opened in 2015 with just 18,000 seats – most stadiums hold 22,000 seats. Marketing strategists found that larger venues rarely sold out, which meant fewer people renewed season tickets, trusting that same-day tickets would be available. The team also uses larger facilities, at Levi Stadium or Stanford Stadium, to build on top of their core audience, a 'casual audience,' in the hope that some might become season ticket holders.

To further entwine its audience, the team supports several fan support clubs, in the European tradition, drawing from communities of Eastern Europeans and Hispanics, as well as 'founding' families and tailgaters. In a 56-page online document called a Brand Constitution, the team says the club's identity represents "a winning heritage, blue-collar, and our passionate and diverse community." Note also a motto, "Unity, Devotion, Heritage," which suggests the kind of personal values you might find in a church, school, social club, or political party. In America, sports have become the Fifth Estate.

Address 1123 Coleman Avenue, San José, CA 95110, www.sjearthquakes.com/avayastadium | Getting there Bus 10, 304 to Coleman & Earthquake | Hours Visit the website for events schedule | Tip For another kind of a game, bring your friends to Beat The Lock Escape Rooms (2131 The Alameda, San José, CA 95110, www.beatthelock.com).

64_ The California Theatre

A culture of gowns and jeans

Downtown San José offers a sense of sophistication mixed with a certain suburban demeanor. Add in utter modernity with the Tech Museum of Innovation, and, a few streets down, the vintage California Theatre. After dark, the theater shines in retro elegance, a masterpiece of movie-house grandeur, recalling an era when the clickety-clack of the projector was the sound of the latest technology. The theater was built in 1927 with elaborate Jazz Age decor by the firm of Weeks and Day, whose designs include Oakland's Fox Theatre and San Francisco's Mark Hopkins Hotel.

The theater fell into disuse in the 1970s and eventually into the hands of the City of San José, which conducted exhaustive restorations in 2004, including the large, vertical, neon *California* sign, and added two Wurlitzer organs. The giant 'blade' marquee, restored to its original size, is defined by a motif of California golden poppies animated with chase lights. The restoration was financed in part by the Packard Humanities fund of Hewlett-Packard. The theater, praised for its acoustics, is home to both Symphony Silicon Valley and Opera San José, which enjoys a national reputation.

A night at the opera in Silicon Valley attracts formally dressed women alongside men in blue jeans and windbreakers, as though never willing to disavow the cultural trappings of codedom. Such is the borderland between San Francisco and San José, and artist perceptions of life outside the arts. The San José opera hosts a unique resident company of artists in the early part of their careers. Each new season offers a range of classics and revivals, and the opera is particularly known for premiering new works. Since its launch in 2002, Symphony Silicon Valley has developed into a world-class institution. Both the opera and the symphony are made even more spectacular because of their home theater. You can rent the theater for your wedding and see your names on the legendary marquee.

Address 345 South 1st Street, San José, CA 95113, +1 (408)792-4542, www.sanjosetheaters.org/
california | Getting there Light rail 902 to Convention Center | Hours See website for schedule |
Tip If you are in the mood to shop for vintage clothing or 1950s furniture, you must stop at Park
Place Vintage (1318 Lincoln Plaza, San José, CA 95125, www.parkplacevintage.com).

65__Cesar Chavez Meeting Hall
Beyond the Grapes of Wrath

One could argue that disruption is in the very soul of the Santa Clara Valley and has been since Junipero Serra introduced Catholicism to the Ohlone Indians, or, on history's flip side, since Cesar Chavez (1927–1993), the revered civil rights activist, began his revolution on behalf of Mexican-American farm workers in the 1950s. While the impact of the Church on California's indigenous populations was disastrous, the Church was supportive of the civil rights efforts of Chavez and gave him space in the Chapel of Our Lady of Guadalupe Church in the Mexican-American neighborhood of Mayfair.

The former chapel was renamed McDonnell Hall, after Father McDonnell, a supporter of Chavez, and was an outpost for voter registration and legislative campaigns. The hall was perhaps most importantly a central meeting place during the 1950s and early 1960s for the Community Service Organization founded by Fred Ross. During the Depression, Ross oversaw the enlightened migrant camp John Steinbeck made famous in *The Grapes of Wrath*. The plight of these migrants inspired his future work with farm workers. The CSO was an early force in training activists like Chavez and Dolores Huerta. When Chavez founded the United Farm Workers, he continued to work out of small meeting halls like this one, now modestly moved to the parking lot behind the newly rebuilt church.

Chavez, the savvy iconoclast, will always be remembered for his tenacity as an organizer, for his fasts, his marches, and his devotion to the cause. He redefined community involvement in his relentless effort to build support, conversation by conversation, encounter by encounter. McDonnell Hall, now a registered historic landmark, is one of several sites in San José that honor the memory of Cesar Chavez, and indirectly the Mexican heritage that shaped the valley long before California was part of America.

Address 2020 East San Antonio Street, San José, CA 95116, www.sanjose.org/listings/
mcdonnell-hall-our-lady-guadalupe-parish | Getting there Bus 23 to Alum Rock & Sunset
or Alum Rock & Checkers, or bus 70 to Jackson & Woodset or Jackson & San Fernando |
Hours Viewable from the outside only | Tip Cesar Chavez home is just three blocks from
the Meeting Hall. It's a private residence not accessible to the public, but there is a
landmark plaque from the City of San José (53 Scharff Avenue, San José, CA 95116).

66_Falafel's Drive In

An immigrant's tale

The trivia question on their website is, "Where in San José can you sit at the same table and eat chips with a technology executive, a nurse, and a stripper?" The answer: Falafel's Drive In on Stevens Creek Boulevard, since 1966 – since anybody can remember – when a Palestinian Catholic family emigrated from Israel and got people addicted to their secret recipe for tahini sauce.

The drive in has been the family's success and struggle. Anton and Zahie Nijmeh opened the place 52 years ago, converting what had been the Snow-White Drive-In into a home base for Middle Eastern specialties. And now the lunch lines just get longer, while the parking is just that much tighter.

The crowd favorite is the $10 combo, with the falafel sandwich and the banana shake. Once you've tasted these delights, you never forget. There is a teacher from Monterey who drives his students up to San José every other week to the Egyptian Museum and planetarium, and then to the drive in. People are just that loyal.

And what about that doyen of dives and diners, Guy Fieri, who has featured this place on his show? People come for that link alone, but they also come for the murals, which ponder the city, with all the local references and icons. You'll need to make several visits to appreciate all the details. The mural is a 600-square-foot tribute to the restaurant, but mostly to San José and surrounding Silicon Valley. On the walls you'll find likenesses of Steve Jobs, Mount Hamilton, the San José City Hall, The Rose Garden, Mission San José, San José Sharks and Earthquakes, Santa Clara University Broncos, and of course portraits of the Nijmeh family. The muralist is Lila Gemellos, who once said, "I see public art murals as the cost-effective art installation which also can do more than beautify. They can educate. They can provoke thought. Murals can, in this case, provoke play."

Address 2301 Stevens Creek Boulevard, San José, CA 95128, +1 (408)294-7886, www.falafelsdrivein.com | Getting there Bus 23, 323 to Stevens Creek & Harold, or bus 23 to Stevens Creek & Cypress | Hours Mon–Sat 10am–8pm, Sun 10am–6pm | Tip For another kind of ethnic food, mostly sweets, visit the Euro Market in Santa Clara (980 El Camino Real, Suite 100, Santa Clara, CA 95050).

67__Falcons Atop City Hall
Love in high places

Since the 1980s, the peregrine falcon has become an urban celebrity, partly for having survived the ravages of DDT in the countryside and recreating themselves in big cities, but also because of the way falcons fetch prey, dropping off the sides of cathedrals, skyscrapers, phone towers, and in Silicon Valley, off the new San José City Hall. Falcons hunt pigeons, owls, swallows, quails, and migrating birds, including small ducks and even bats, and eat them while in flight. Incidentally, falcons have come to favor hunting in the night light in cities, shooting down in a 'stoop,' hitting targets at up to 240 mph.

In the mid-1970s, there were only two known breeding pairs of peregrine falcons in California. In response, the Santa Cruz Predatory Bird Research Group set out to help restore the population. One of their first successful efforts came in 2006, when they contracted with officials at the then new 18-story San José City Hall. Richard Meier, best known for his Barcelona Museum of Contemporary Art and Getty Center in Los Angeles, designed the striking new building, including the rotunda with the transparent dome, reminiscent of a glass cathedral.

It was completed in 2005 and the next year became a haven for two peregrines named Clara and José. Nesting boxes were built on the top floor and eventually the couple moved in. They had three kids. In 2011, Clara remarried, to Esteban Colbert (named after Stephen Colbert) who was finally driven off by Fernando El Cohete (Fernando the Rocket). They had three more offspring: two girls, Cielo and Meyye, and a boy named Mercury. Clara and her partners have become avian Kardashians with their own Facebook page and a live stream.

You can glimpse Clara and her family from the top floor of the 4th Street parking garage or the 8th floor of the Martin Luther King, Jr. Library, which has a high-powered telescope.

Address 200 East Santa Clara Street, San José, CA 95113, +1 (408)535-4800, www.sanjoseca.gov | Getting there Bus 22, 23, 522 to Santa Clara & 5th, or bus 64, 65, 81 to 7th & Santa Clara | Hours City Hall, Mon–Fri, 8am–5pm | Tip The Black Power Statue at nearby Olympic Park depicts two Olympic medalists and San José State University students Tommie Smith and John Carlos who, at the 1968 summer games in Mexico City, raised their fists in the Black Power salute as the American national anthem played (Olympic Park, San José, CA 95112).

68 Google's Transit Village
An end to car-centricity

Many of the major companies in the valley are expanding beyond California, some more quickly outside the state than within. Apple is building a $1-billion campus in Austin. Google will open a $1-billion global headquarters in lower Manhattan, its Hudson Square campus. Both companies are adding offices and data centers across the country.

Within the Valley, Google has been acquiring property in Mountain View, including a $1-billion business park. But it's in San José where Google is undertaking one of the more interesting experiments in using corporate space in the region by building a 'transit village,' a 50-acre urban habitat to be filled with shops, restaurants, parks, and office space for up to 20,000 workers. It will be open to the public.

It will also be located close to Diridon Train Station. Diridon is an Italian Renaissance Revival-style depot on Cahill Street downtown. It serves Amtrak, Caltrain, the ACE train, and eventually BART. Diridon is set to become the Grand Central of the West Coast, and the lynchpin of Google's village. The land for this project is both public and private – as of this writing, it's largely vacant lots, homes and industrials sites. The city has given its blessing; polls reflect community support. Progressive planning experts applaud the idea of constructing high buildings downtown near a transit hub, which helps steer urban evolution away from a car-centric culture.

The existing Googleplex has an on-campus Google Visitor's Center at 1911 Landings Drive in Mountain View, but it is only open to employees and their guests. Buildings are surrounded by Charleston Park, a city park that's open to the public. If you can visit the Googleplex campus, you'll notice the multicolored custom Gbikes. Google employees use them to cruise from building to building. Google maintains roughly 1,100 free two-wheelers.

Address 165 Cahill Street, San José, CA 95110, www.diridonsj.org/saag | Getting there Caltrain to Diridon | Hours Unrestricted | Tip For another kind of competition, visit Twin Creeks Sports Complex in Sunnyvale, where you'll get 60 acres of sports, fun, and events (969 Caribbean Drive, Sunnyvale, CA 94089, www.twin-creeks.com).

69 — The Japanese American Museum

Histories from an American gulag

In the months after the Japanese attack on Pearl Harbor on December 7, 1941, old animosities in America caught fire. Since the late 19th century, Asian immigrants, notably the Chinese, suffered the slings and arrows of public mistrust. Now, the public claimed just cause and focused their fear and loathing on Japanese Americans. Add to bigotry stories in 1937 about Japanese Army atrocities in Nanking, where nearly half the city's population of 600,000 was brutally murdered.

In February 1942, President Roosevelt signed Executive Order 9066, which authorized the incarceration of more than 120,000 people living along the West Coast. Of those, 70,000 were American citizens. The order defied studies arguing that in the event of war with Japan, Japanese Americans were unlikely to become a fifth column. In an operation reminiscent of Nazi roundups in the 'bloodlands' of Eastern Europe, entire families of farmers, doctors, and teachers were hustled out of their houses and businesses, which were then sold for little or else looted. All assets were frozen. The people, including children and the elderly, carrying only what could fit in a few suitcases, were sent off to more than a dozen concentration camps in largely western states. There they remained imprisoned until 1944. They lived in barracks, often with strangers and with no bathrooms but communal latrines with no partitions.

This tragic history is captured in great detail in a unique museum in San José in the middle of Japantown. Exhibits include stories from immigrants in the 19th century, and also tools and farm equipment and a replica of a barracks room at the Tule Lake Segregation Center. A total of 33,000 Japanese Americans served in the US military during the war, and approximately 800 were killed in action. The volunteer docents at the museum may offer insights and personal stories of incarceration.

Address 535 North 5th Street, San José, CA 95112, +1 (408)294-3138, www.jamsj.org, mail@jamsj.org | **Getting there** Bus 65 to 6th & Empire, bus 66 to 1st & Empire or 1st & Hawthorne, or Light Rail 901, 902 to Japantown / Ayer | **Hours** Thu – Sun noon – 4pm | **Tip** The popular Obon Festival to honor the spirits of the ancestors happens every summer in Japantown, starting at José Buddhist Church Betsuin (640 North 5th Street, San José, CA 95112, www.jtown.org/events).

70__Kelley Park
The future of the past

One of the illusions of Silicon Valley is that it's a monolithic Bay Area suburb with no particular history, defined merely by a few vast tech companies and myriad little startups. And at the center of it all: Stanford University, the Castle on the Hill of Silicon Valley, home of the era's holy grail. That's one truth-myth. Another is that Silicon Valley is a pseudonym for a collection of small towns, once farmer bergs, stretching from Burlingame to San José. From that angle, these disparate little communities form the true heart of the valley. You think of downtown Las Gatos, with its historic Main Street, that was once provincial and now increasingly worldly.

Or you might think of Kelley Park, just south of downtown San José. The park is well known locally for Happy Hollow Park and Zoo, a surprising and fun feature for young kids that includes a modest, but well-cared-for collection of small animals – red-ruffed lemurs, meerkats, and a red panda, among others. Other kid-friendly attractions include a gentle rollercoaster, a carousel, puppet shows, and also educational events, including classes, and sleepovers. Kids can learn how to be junior animal keepers and rangers at spring and summer camps.

And then there's the rest of Kelley Park, which is known as History Park, designed as an indoor/outdoor museum to honor local heritages. Of note are the Japanese gardens, the Portuguese Historical Museum, a Viet museum, a Chinese American museum, and an early electronics museum. These places are part of a kind of gated, studio sound stage, built in 1971 to look like a small town at the turn of the last century. There are 29 buildings and landmarks that are either replicas or original buildings moved to the spot. To feel the small-town roots of Silicon Valley, visit the park on a weekday, when these nostalgic streets are often empty. You have the sense of being thrust into a former reality, that old domain where people meet and connect, face-to-face.

Address 1300 Senter Road, San José, CA 95112, +1 (408)794-7275, www.sanjose.org/listings/kelley-park | **Getting there** Bus 73 to Senter & Kelley Park | **Hours** Daily 8am–dusk | **Tip** For tasty pho noodles, visit Binh Minh Vietnamese Restaurant just 0.3 miles away from the park (999 Story Road, San José, CA 95122).

71__MACLA
Make/See Art Here

San José has gathered together a diverse array of arts attractions downtown, including the San José Museum of Art, the Tech Museum, and the Museum of Quilts and Textiles. One of the lesser known but increasingly important spots in this cluster in the SoFA District is the Movimiento de Arte y Cultura Latino Americano, known by its acronym MACLA. The slogan, *Make Art Here*, emblazoned above the bright purple building entrance, suggests the center's community identity as an important incubator for Latino/Chicano arts initiatives. MACLA is also a center for music, performance, and arts education, as well as changing visual exhibits featuring international and local artists.

The intersections of art and contemporary politics have been a vital feature of Latino arts since Diego Rivera, and the work at MACLA similarly reflects a serious engagement with issues such as immigration, gender equality, education, and, above all, the drive to bring people together. On any night you might find a high school youth arts showcase and open mic in one studio, while a Cuban dance band backs up a dramatic performance in the theatre space. The Chicano Biennial is one of the most popular changing exhibits showcasing cutting-edge Chicano/Latino art. The recent '7th Xicanx Biennial: Muxeres Rising' was a multi-generational exploration of Latino women's work. First Friday Fiesta nights, when the space is open late, is a chance to 'Meet, Make, Move' with musicians and dancers from the Latino diaspora.

Connected to the museum philosophically, though not physically, are a number of nearby murals created by Empire 7 Studios (aka E7S). What started as an out-of-the-way gallery in Japantown has spilled on to the streets throughout the area. The murals have helped to revitalize the neighborhood, and can be found online (www.codeforsanjose.com/heartofthevalley).

Address 510 South 1st Street, San José, CA 95113, +1 (408)998-2783, www.maclaarte.org, info@maclaare.org | Getting there Caltrain to San José Diridon, or VTA Bus 66, 68, 82 to 1st & Reed or 2nd & William | Hours Wed–Thu noon–7pm, Fri–Sun noon–5pm | Tip Café Stritch just a block away is a great place to relax with live jazz music and craft cocktails (374 South 1st Street, San José, CA 95113, www.cafestritch.com).

72__Municipal Rose Garden
Olfactory paradise in Florabunda Ville

Due west of downtown San José, south of 82 and east of 280, you come to an old and distinguished neighborhood known as the Rose Garden. This was once land focused on pear and prune orchards, and then in the late 1930s divided up into residential lots that sold for $5 each. For years, the architectural theme was Tudor Revival, or as the British would say, mock Tudor. Variations included Cotswold, otherwise known as the Storybook style, noted for steep gables, arched doorways, and walls lined with stone or brick. Some of the original Cotswold bungalows remain, although many were torn down and replaced with a hodgepodge of echoes and revivals.

The Rose Garden District runs along either side of Naglee Avenue. This is where you will find the rucian Egyptian Museum (see ch. 75), the historic Hoover Theater, and the San José Municipal Rose Garden, the winner of America's Best Rose Garden Award. The garden, which opened in 1937, is 5.5 acres, filling up several blocks surrounded by a fence. There are splendid redwood stands, a large fountain, a delightful arbor, and then the rose beds themselves; 4,000 rose shrubs and 189 varieties create an olfactory paradise with many varieties of Floribunda, including such rarities as a 1968 *DeRuiter Europeana*. Particularly fragrant roses include the Dick Clark, Wild Blue Yonder, Koko Loko, and the Secret Hybrid Tea Rose. No matter the time of year, there's always something in bloom.

The garden ambience is reminiscent of Seurat's *Sunday Afternoon in the Park* – sans the lake – and at the same time very much in the style of Northern California with blanketed lovers, the roar of a muscle car, brides and grooms, different accents, and the occasional smell of barbecue. The garden otherwise guards its olfactory pleasures, so dogs are not allowed and neither is alcohol or smoking. And of course, you can't pick the flowers.

Address Dana Avenue and Naglee Avenue, San José, CA 95112, +1 (408)794-7274, www.sanJoséca.gov/Facilities/Facility/Details/74 | **Getting there** Bus 61, 62 to Naglee & Dana | **Hours** Daily 8am–30 minutes before sunset | **Tip** Antiques Colony is a wonderful store where you can find old prints, antique home decor, or anything old and eclectic, as well as mid-century wares (1881 West San Carlos Street, San José, CA 95182, www.antiquescolony.com).

73 New Almaden Mining Historic District

The dark era of quicksilver

In the great American mythos of the West, rugged individualist gold miners trudged into the wilderness to strike it rich. But the truer, less-known story of mining, for gold especially, is one of environmental destruction and immigrant communities toiling for the enrichment of foreign investors. Nowhere is this story more prominent than at the New Almaden Mine where, between 1850 and 1890, more than 70 million dollars' worth of red cinnabar was mined and heated to create mercury, a critical material in the extraction of gold from ore. New Almaden was monetarily the most lucrative mine works in California.

New Almaden attracted miners from Mexico, England, and Chile, and Chinese laborers under the iron hand of Eustace Baron, whose British company was notorious for its corruption. The streets and homes of the mine workers vanished long ago, and New Almaden is a now a wild enclave of hiking trails dotted with sealed mine entrances and industrial ruins. The beautifully preserved Casa Grande, once the mine headquarters and now the New Almaden Quicksilver Mining Museum, displays details of Santa Clara life in the 19th century and the quicksilver saga.

New Almaden also features prominently in the literature of California. Mary Hallock Foote, the wife of the Almaden resident engineer from 1876, wrote and illustrated *A California Mining Camp*, a popular series about a Victorian woman's adventures in the rough and tumble West. Years later Wallace Stegner in his Pulitzer Prize-winning novel, *Angle of Repose*, fictionalized her account of life at Almaden. The juxtaposition of Eastern norms on the wild reality of Western life, has since become a defining meme in the literature of the American West. Stegner taught at Stanford for several decades and his legacy continues.

Address New Almaden Quicksilver Museum, 21350 Almaden Road, San José, CA 95120, +1 (408)323-1107, www.newalmaden.org | **Getting there** By car, take CA-85 to Almaden Expressway exit and follow to Almaden Road | **Hours** Mon, Tue, Fri noon–4pm, Sat & Sun 10am–4pm | **Tip** At Hacienda Cemetery at New Almaden you can find the grave of the left arm of one Bert Barrett. When he was 13 years old, a shotgun blew off almost half of his left arm, and it's buried at the cemetery. His body is buried at Memorial Hill Oak Cemetery 11 miles away (21480 Bertram Road, New Almaden, San José, CA 95120, www.californiapioneers.com/visit/hacienda-cemetery).

74_Playa to Paseo
Burning Man art in San José

The Burning Man Festival is held every August in Nevada's Black Rock Desert, 120 miles northeast of Reno. The festival is about community and art, and each event is sparked by a particular theme, such as 'Fertility 2.0,' 'Da Vinci's Workshop,' and 'Radical Ritual.' The festival's signature conclusion is the burning of the festival temple, as well as a wooden effigy of The Man.

In an effort to retain the ephemeral, interactive art installations and sculptures created for the festival in public view, the Burning Man Foundation and the City of San José have established Playa to Paseo. The pieces are on loan to the city and can be found in the Civic Center Area of San José. The technological innovation that goes into the creation of many of these art pieces is widely appreciated in the valley, not to mention the fact that young techies are among the most ardent attendees at the festival. One recent favorite, *The Sonic Runway*, exemplified the techie/hipster aesthetic of the project. A series of arches form a runway through which you can walk with music playing along the way, visually rippling through the arches.

Another recent favorite is the *Tara Mechani*, a 15-foot-tall figurative sculpture that re-imagines the Buddhist female deity Tara as both jeweled bronze goddess and futuristic robot. The elegance of the piece, by artist Dana Albany, is achieved through reused industrial objects. It has a delicacy and beauty that captures a spiritual presence.

Using common materials in uncommon ways is a theme also echoed in a recent piece, *Ursa Mater*, or mother bear. This sculpture of a bear and two cubs, uses 200,000 pennies to create fur. The effect is both surprisingly natural and strangely pun-like. The bear is the state emblem of California, and whether the artists meant to suggest that all our symbols are made of money is a matter of speculation.

Address Various, San José, www.sanjoseculture.org | **Getting there** See website for locations | **Hours** Unrestricted | **Tip** For a tasty cocktail selection, stop by the Paper Plane (72 South 1st Street, San José, CA 95113, www.paperplanesj.com).

75__ The Rosicrucian Egyptian Museum

Home to an ancient order of Christian mystics

On a long, sleepy block in the heart of San José's Garden District, you will find The Rosicrucian Egyptian Museum, otherwise known as Rosicrucian Park. The park fills up an entire block and includes a multistory exhibit hall, a research library, a planetarium, a Rosicrucian temple and alchemy museum, a labyrinth, and elaborate gardens and pools, along with a life-sized Senet game, a 5,000-year-old board game. The walled gardens are reminiscent of those geometrically designed spaces that you find in Seville and Granada, both cities along the same latitude as Silicon Valley.

The exhibit hall offers the largest collection of mummies and Egyptian artifacts on the West Coast. Staff members regularly travel to Egypt to update the exhibits, which feature a full-sized reproduction of a rough-cut stone tomb. Notable artifacts include papyrus documents, cylinder seals, and a large monolith with Hammurabi's Code of Laws. There's also an alchemy exhibit with a reproduction of an alchemist's workshop. The museum plans to make this the largest alchemy museum in the world.

Rosicrucian Park was founded in 1927 by the Ancient and Mystical Order of Rosae Crucis (AMORC), symbolized by the rose and the cross. AMORC dates back to the early 1600s and is based on a series of manifestos documenting the esoteric nature of the Rosicrucian path. It currently claims some 80,000 adherents worldwide and this park in San José is also home to their North American Grand Lodge. The order is devoted to the study of metaphysical laws and ancient philosophies, hence the connection to Egypt. Rosicrucians claim a deep sense of connection to the divine, a connection with no intermediaries. Famous Rosicrucians include Benjamin Franklin, Abraham Lincoln, Isaac Newton, Leonardo Da Vinci, Walt Disney, and Ronald Reagan.

Address 1660 Park Avenue, San José, CA 95191, +1 (408)947-3635, www.egyptianmuseum.org | **Getting there** Bus 81 to Park & Randall or Park & Naglee | **Hours** Wed–Fri 9am–5pm, Sat & Sun 10am–6pm | **Tip** The nearby Seeing Things Gallery hosts monthly art shows and features zines, books, magazines, T-shirts, tote bags, and cards on their brightly colored shelves (751 West San Carlos Street, San José, CA 95126, www.seeingthingsgallery.com).

76__San José Museum of Quilts & Textiles

Living in the material world

Whatever patterns may come to mind when you think of quilting, it's worth noting that this is definitely not your grandma's quilt museum. This museum presents textiles that expand our notions of the material world, quite literally. All that is made of fiber, from ancient weavings to contemporary paper sculpture, are among the exhibits.

Since 2010, the museum has hosted the International TECHstyle Art Biennial (ITAB), which presents work by artists who employ various technologies in creating fiber-based work. Using Silicon Valley's resources on the tech side of the work has helped to attract a global community of artists to the event. The connection between textile manufacturing and what would become computer technology dates to the early 19th century, when Joseph Marie Jacquard (1752–1834), a French weaver from Lyon, used punch cards to develop automated looms to create complex patterns. Textiles were the first material to be widely produced in the Industrial Revolution and continue to reflect digital technologies. Exploring the tension between hand-made versus machine-made textiles is an ongoing theme among artists here.

The museum is equally devoted to the social history of quilting. The Bay Area was a center of the resurgence of quilting arts in the 1970s, and the work of artists like Miriam Nathan Roberts are featured here. Through the Social Justice Sewing Academy, an arts education project for local students, the museum teaches sewing and promotes quilting as a means of youth engagement.

As one of the most ancient and tangible mediums of design, textiles carry profound cultural messages. The collection of textiles at the museum include tribal and traditional works. For a small fee, aficionados can schedule a private tour of the archived collection.

Address 520 South 1st Street, San José, CA 95113, +1 (408)971-0323, www.sjquiltmuseum.org, info@sjquiltmuseum.org | Getting there Light Rail 902 to Convention Center | Hours Wed–Fri 11am–4pm, Sat & Sun 11am–3pm | Tip The Lace Museum in Santa Clara is much smaller, but also well worth visiting (552 South Murphy Avenue, Sunnyvale, CA 94086, www.thelacemuseum.org).

77__Sikh Gurdwara Sahib

A temple of equality

The strands of global influence that meet in Silicon Valley are both subtle and highly visible. The San José Sikh Gurdwara, or temple, built on a hillside overlooking the valley in east San José, is definitely visible. At 90,000 square feet, this temple is the largest *gurdwara* in North America and was built between 1999 and 2011.

The façades in Gujarati and Mughal styles, with scalloped archways, porticoes, and domes, bring a distinctly South Asian look to the landscape. Other signatures of Sikh architecture include the *Nishan Sahib,* a Sikh banner, flying high above the domed rooftops, the spacious open central hall, and the lack of statuary.

Originating in the early 1500s in the Punjab region near the border with Pakistan, the Sikh faith was founded by Guru Nanak. It shares with Hinduism a belief in karma but departs in holding that all humans are equal in stature, part of one divine unity. Adherents practice selfless service and "strive for justice and the prosperity of all."

There are more than 20 million Sikhs worldwide, many recognizable by the turban worn by men to cover their uncut hair. While Sikhs have historically struggled as a minority in their Hindu/Muslim homeland, the Sikh community in San José has flourished. Part of the larger South Asian population in the Santa Clara valley, the Sikhs here are particularly open to public visits to the gurdwara, which has caught on as a local attraction.

Regardless of creed, one can share a free vegetarian meal, prepared in the community kitchen, or *langar*, and then eaten together seated on the floor as a symbol of the equality of all people. A daily schedule of sung prayers, or *kirtan*, often accompanied by music, is also presented. You can stroll through the simple but contemplative grounds, including the water fountains and pools that line the porticoes. The view of the valley is almost divine.

Address 3636 Gurdwara Avenue, San José, CA 95148, +1 (408)274-9373, www.sikhgurudwarasj.org | Getting there Bus 39 to Murillo & Chaboya | Hours See website for hours and events | Tip Another beautiful sanctuary and a place to respite is the Cathedral Basilica of St. Joseph in San José. The original church was built in 1803 as the first non-mission parish in California (80 South Market Street, San José, CA 95113, www.stjosephcathedral.org).

78_Veggielution

An experiment in urban farming

Urban farming has become a *cause célèbre*, yet fully functioning urban farms remain rare. In San José, the real thing is Veggielution, a six-acre community farm, spread out underneath the flyovers of Highways 101 and 280. This is just east of downtown, in the Mayfair neighborhood. Veggielution, and the Emma Prusch Farm Park adjacent to it, are among the last vestiges of those eras before Santa Clara Valley turned to Silicon, when this area was known as the Valley of Heart's Delight because of the warm weather, fertile soil, and persistent breezes that sweetened the fruit orchards.

In 1962, a landowner and farmer Emma Prusch, with the can-do smile of Eleanor Roosevelt, donated 86 acres of her farm to the city to encourage the memory of San José's agricultural character. The farm park includes a Victorian farmhouse, flower gardens, a classic red barn, fruit orchards, picnic areas, a children's playground, wandering peacocks, and a real community garden open to members only. Next to that is Veggielution, with its own organic gardens, where the public is invited to volunteer and experience urban farming first-hand. There is also a beautiful wisteria-covered bio-dome.

The park is always abuzz with festivals, but most importantly it serves as a conduit of relatively inexpensive fresh food to one of the poorer neighborhoods in Silicon Valley, where rates of obesity and diabetes are high. In the 1950s, Cesar Chavez held community meetings here (see ch. 65), and now the neighborhood has become a magnet for a new class of migrant worker: the lettuce pickers of the tech industry, doing menial jobs around the digital estate. Nearly half the residents of Mayfair are foreign-born, roughly three-quarters are Latino and one-quarter Asian, mostly Vietnamese. The promise of Veggielution is in its ability to encourage civic engagement. Take part in the community potluck on Saturdays.

Address 647 King Road, San José, CA 95116, +1 (408)753-6705, www.veggielution.org |
Getting there Bus 12, 22, 77 to King & Chaucer | Hours Mon – Sat 8am – 5pm | Tip The
annual Prusch Farm Park Mountain Music Festival takes place in the park in October,
with live entertainment, hay rides, and farm animals to pet (647 King Road, San José,
CA 95116, www.pruschfarmpark.org/mountain-music-fest.html).

79__Victory Stand
The 'silent protest' in Speed City

San José State University, founded in 1857, was the state's first school of public higher education. The campus, in downtown San José, has cultivated a reputation based partly on the gritty, 'never say die' spirit of its Division 1 football team, the Spartans. Sports are a big deal at State. So is diversity, and respect for diversity. Freshman orientation courses include a class on 'micro aggression' and, if you miss the class, you're blocked from registration.

The school's focus on diversity is symbolized in a 23-foot-tall sculpture depicting that iconic moment at the 1968 Olympics in Mexico City when two SJS track stars, Tommie Smith and John Carlos, stood on the winner's podium to accept Gold and Bronze respectively in the 200-meter race. They raised their arms in a symbol of Black pride, in what Smith later described as a "silent protest."

Smith and Carlos stepped onto the podium wearing black socks and no shoes – to symbolize black poverty. Smith carried a box with an olive tree sapling as an emblem of peace. Carlos wore beads around his neck in honor of all those blacks who had been lynched, or killed "and that no-one said a prayer for."

Smith and Carlos were inspired by the sociologist Harry Edwards, a longtime figure in Bay Area sports, and a mentor to former SF 49er quarterback Colin Kaepernick.

Smith later commented, "If I win, I am American, not a Black American. But if I did something bad, then they would say I am a negro… Black America will understand what we did tonight." Both returned from the Olympics to San José, where their reception was mixed, to the sorrow of Smith and Carlos. The track program, once known as Speed City, was abandoned in 1988.

The creator of the *Victory Stand* is a San Francisco artist Rigo 23, known by his murals and political art. The statue is made of steel, fiberglass and ceramic tiles and was dedicated to SJSU in 2005.

Address Paseo De San Antonio, San José State University, South 7th Street, San José, CA 95112, +1 (408)924-1000, www.sjsu.edu | **Getting there** Bus 63, 64, 65, 72, 73, 81 to San Fernando & 5th, or bus 201 to 4th & San Carlos | **Hours** Unrestricted | **Tip** Classical music lovers must visit Ira F. Brilliant Center for Beethoven Studies, located at the library at SJSU on the 4th floor (One Washington Square, San José, CA 95192, www.sjsu.edu/beethoven).

80__ Winchester Mystery House
An early ghost in the machine

Among the great ancestors of the semi-automatic rifle was the repeating rifle, first developed in Austria and then refined in America, beginning in the mid-1800s. Early brands included the Winchester rifle, a four-foot-long, lever-action repeater. During the Civil War, the United States Army was reluctant to buy the gun because it didn't trust the new technology, but the rifle became increasingly popular among the public, particularly pioneers. Hence, the gun became known as 'the gun that won the West.' Ironically, it was also used in the Battle of the Little Bighorn.

Oliver Winchester (1810–1880) was a Connecticut businessman and a venture capitalist who, in 1857, acquired a failing gun company with a brilliant engineer, and launched the Winchester Repeating Arms Company. He made his son, William, treasurer, and then died in 1880. A year later William died, and his wife Sarah inherited today's equivalent of $500 million. Sarah was a round-faced, unusually well-educated woman from New Haven, CT. Her father earned a small fortune making ambulances. She and William had one child who died after 40 days.

The deaths of child and husband led Sarah to flee to Europe. Three years later she returned and sought out a famous Boston psychic who told her she was cursed by the spirits of all the people killed by the Winchester rifle. He suggested she devote her life to building a house under permanent construction as a way to trick and trap her tormentors. She promptly moved to San José, bought an eight-room farmhouse and spent the next 38 years developing a maze of hundreds of rooms, twisting hallways, stairways leading nowhere, and a door that opened to a one-story drop to the pavement below. Work went on 24 hours a day. At late night séances, she received instructions for the next days' work. Helen Mirren portrayed her in the 2018 film *Winchester*.

Address 525 South Winchester Boulevard, San José, CA 95128, www.winchestermysteryhouse.com | Getting there Bus 60 to Winchester & Olsen | Hours See website for seasonal hours and tours | Tip The Tech Museum of Innovation in San José, or The Tech, is an interactive museum for the whole family to learn about science and technology (201 South Market Street, San José, CA 95113, www.thetech.org).

81_LJB Farms
Down under Silicon Valley

Louie Bonino is a 77-year-old farmer in the San Martin Valley, northwest of Gilroy, at the foot of the Santa Cruz Mountain. After all these years in the sun, his skin has turned the color of mahogany. He had back surgery not long ago and now uses a cane. Otherwise, he's looking good. He's kept his humor, his friends, and his perspective. "I like my lifestyle," he'll tell you, sitting on a tall, wooden chair outside his elaborate vegetable market filled with just-picked corn, tomatoes, beans, squash, cucumbers, strawberries, and onions. He'll put 30 acres to pumpkins in the fall. Plus dried fruits. That's just half his business, and customers come from as far as San Francisco and Monterey. His other crop is seeds, which he exports to the UK.

Yes, he likes his lifestyle and the food, of course, despite it being a slim-margin business that shifts like a kite in the wind, and despite a future in the unwitting hands of the fast-expanding digital class of development engineers, product managers, and data warehouse architects, Silicon Valley's 21st-century factory workers, who are relentlessly buying up the old farms. They like the 20-acre farms, but the fields once devoted to milk cows and chickens aren't their thing. The land is disappearing under the waves of subdivisions, where children think food is grown in supermarkets.

In the early 1980s, Louie might see five cars a day pass his market. Now, the cars rarely stop. He comes from families of Italian men and Swiss women. His great grandfather came from Turin, got to Illinois, took a job as a coal miner and then a copper miner in Utah, and finally, in 1917, he reached Gilroy. His dad had the first caterpillar tractor in this part of the valley.

Louie's two sons, Russ and Brent, the Bonino fourth-generation farmers, are making sure the family farm will continue to enrich the Valley of the Heart's Delight.

Address 585 Fitzgerald Avenue, San Martin, CA 95046, +1 (408)842-9755, www.ljbfarms.com, barn@ljbfarms.com | **Getting there** By car, take US-101 to exit 360, continue straight to Fitzgerald Avenue | **Hours** Early spring–Dec 24, daily 9am–6pm | **Tip** Nearby in Gilroy, the Garlic City Cafe offers tasty lunch options. Try the garlic cheeseburger and the garlic ice cream for dessert – if you dare (7461 Monterey Street, Gilroy, CA 95020, www.garliccitycafe.com).

82__ Wings of History Air Museum

Finding the Lindy in every man

The Hiller Aviation Museum in San Mateo is a state-of-the-art museum, designed to wow and to challenge. But there's a second air museum that is very much worth a visit, the Wings of History Air Museum behind the San Martin small-plane airport. It's as though your grandfather took you to his garage one day and, for the first time, showed you what he'd been working on for all these years.

The Wings of History Museum is focused on the toil, especially the hobbyist in his backyard machine shop, learning to wing it, literally and figuratively. Exhibits include many experimental planes developed in the early to mid-20th century, including hidden gems like a 1932 Penguin, designed not to fly but to train new pilots how to taxi. A 1940 Security Airster was a single engine plane, first developed in 1932 with folding wings. And a 1957 Dobbins SimCopter was a highly imaginative attempt to combine a car with a helicopter. It flew briefly.

The Wing of History Museum's two hangars house 20 full-sized, mostly antique planes and 147 models – this is an airplane modeler's paradise. There's also a 'prop shop,' the only one west of the Mississippi certified by the FAA, which repairs and manufacturer wooden propellers. They make four or five a year.

The airport also offers classes with topics like 'History of the Flying Wing Airplane Development into the B-2 Stealth Bomber.' Friends of the museum are building a full-sized glider, and volunteers are encouraged to join the effort. There's a library with 4,000 hardbound books, offering biographies, as well as flight manuals on civil, commercial, and military aircraft, along with airframe maintenance manuals. Museum curators are friendly and informative and if they're not too busy, they'll provide tours on the spot.

Address 12777 Murphy Avenue, San Martin, CA 95046, +1 (408)683-2290, www.wingsofhistory.org | Getting there Take US-101 to exit 362, merging onto East San Martin Avenue to Murphy Avenue | Hours Tue & Thu 10am–3pm, Sat & Sun 11am–4pm | Tip For wine tasting and a bocce ball game, visit picturesque Clos La Chance Winery (1 Hummingbird Lane, San Martin, CA 95046, www.clos.com).

83 Eichler Houses

Joseph Eichler left no room for bigots

California's most influential architects include Frank Gehry, with the Walt Disney Concert Hall and his home in Santa Monica, as well as Frederick Emmons and A. Quincy Jones who, besides their own commissions, collaborated to design thousands of homes in hundreds of styles for the legendary developer Joseph Eichler (1900–1974).

Eichler was an oddball genius, a gregarious, button-down moralist in Brooks Brothers suits who, until middle age, worked in his wife's family egg and butter distribution business. When that was sold, Eichler invested in construction. He saw a market for simple, modern-looking homes for 'common people' who could afford tract homes costing $10,000. His first house was built in 1949. There are Eichler homes from Palm Springs to Sacramento, but the highest concentration, some 700 homes, is in the Highlands in San Mateo County, a hilly neighborhood across Highway 280 from the Crystal Springs reservoir.

For mid-century modern aficionados, the Eichlers are not just homes but collector's items. The style is a low, airy, horizontal look tuned to what Wright called "a companion to the horizon." Homes were made of brick and wood and were hidden from the street. But at the back of the houses, there were walls of glass. The Eichler signature included open-air atriums, slab foundations, post-and-beam construction, flat roofs, mahogany paneling, built-in furniture, and heating through the floors, which critics claim often doesn't work.

Eichler, the son of German-Jewish parents, was famously progressive. Years before the laws were changed in California, he established non-discrimination sales policies and once told owners worried about an integrated neighborhood, "If, as you claim, this will destroy property values, I could lose millions. You should be ashamed of yourselves for wasting your time and mine with such pettiness."

Address San Mateo Highlands, San Mateo, CA 94402 | **Getting there** By car, take I-280 to exit 34 | **Hours** Viewable from the outside only | **Tip** Try the happy hour at The Field Club. Nice cocktails, and the ribs are very good too (742 Polhemus Road, San Mateo, CA 94402, www.thefieldclub.net).

84 Agnews Insane Asylum
A life among insane

The first 'lunatic asylum' in the United States opened in Williamsburg, Virginia in 1769. Eighty years later, in 1850, the first lunatic asylum in San Francisco opened in the hold of the *Euphemia*, a 90-foot brig used as a holding tank for street people who appeared to be of dubious mind. A year later, the state's first psychiatric hospital opened in Stockton, and so began the golden age of asylums, both private and public. Of course, protocols were primitive. Patients were sometimes forcibly sterilized as the notion of eugenics slowly took hold.

In 1888, California opened the third insane asylum in the farmland north of San José. It became known as the Agnews State Mental Hospital and acquired a reputation for progressive policies, including a 'cottage system' where small one- and two-story cottages replaced large, multi-story buildings. Each cottage held a particular kind of patient. There were no bars on the windows and, except in extreme circumstances, restraints weren't used.

By the 1970s, mental illness was distinguished from mental disabilities. Agnews was renamed a development center and focused on patients with epilepsy, cerebral palsy, mental retardation, and autism. A Stanford professor found out in the late 1980s that his son, a patient at Agnews, had been filled with psychotropic medicines, sometimes sent into a closet for his behavior, and otherwise treated as though he would always have the mind of a toddler. This 'therapy' was before doctors understood that autistic people are very well aware of the world around them.

In 1996, the state closed the center and sold the property to Sun Microsystems for $51 million. Sun was acquired by Oracle Corporation in 2010. The campus, built in Mediterranean Revival architecture and landscaped with palms, pepper trees, and vast lawns, is now used as a research and development facility and conference center.

Address 2150 Agnew Road, Santa Clara, CA 95054, +1 (408)615-3140, www.dds.ca.gov/ Agnews | Getting there Bus 60, 140, 321, 330, 827 to Mission College & Burton | Hours Unrestricted from the outside only | Tip The Agnews Historic Cemetery and Museum, where patients and staff of the asylum are remembered, is located nearby (1250 Hope Drive, Santa Clara, CA 95054, www.santaclaraca.gov).

85__The Intel Museum
The work of street fighters

Silicon Valley is named after that shiny, bluish, brittle crystalline, which is the second most abundant element in the Earth's crust – after oxygen. Its properties include the ability to conduct electrical currents. It was the Santa Clara company, Intel, in 1971 that created the world's first commercial microprocessor chip, which in turn became, among other things, the brain of the personal computer. Intel, the name a combination of 'integrated' and 'electricity,' was founded with $250 in 1968 by group of "street fighters," in the words of a physicist named Robert Noyce (1927–1990), once nicknamed the 'Mayor of Silicon Valley.' He and Gordon Moore, an engineer who calls himself the 'accidental entrepreneur,' along with the 'management scientist' named Andrew Grove (1936–2016), created arguably the valley's most distinguished tech company.

Incidentally, it was Gordon Moore who established Moore's law, not a physical law, but a dramatic prediction, made in 1965, that the number of components per integrated circuit would double each year. He revised his forecast in later years, as technological change slowed and saturation set in.

One of the management signatures of Intel came from Noyce's leadership style. He disdained corporate cars and jets, and even reserved parking spaces, and he really did treat employees as family. That inclination, to be open and reach out to the community, is reflected in the Intel Museum, which tells the story of silicon and the chip, and the process by which microprocessors are made, including wafer deposition, lithography, etching, cutting, and completion.

Few of the other big companies in the valley offer much in the way of public access, much less through a true museum. The Intel Museum is small, free, and takes about an hour to go through, and you can arrange for a guided tour if you'd like more insights and explanations.

Address 2200 Mission College Boulevard, Santa Clara, CA 95054, +1 (408)765 5050, www.intel.com/content/www/us/en/company-overview/intel-museum.html, museum@intel.com | **Getting there** Bus 60, 321, 330, 827 to Mission College & Wyatt, or Mission College & Burton | **Hours** Mon–Fri 9am–6pm, Sat 10am–5pm | **Tip** Do you love video games? The Digital Game Museum has preserved the history of all your favorites (3553 Ryder Street, Santa Clara, CA 95051, www.digitalgamemuseum.org).

86 __ Levi's Stadium
The roar of the hoi polloi

Levi's Stadium opened in Santa Clara in 2014 and was named after Levi Strauss & Company, a business pillar in San Francisco since 1853. Among those who have worn Levi's clothing: Albert Einstein. In 2013, the company agreed to pay $220 million to the city of Santa Clara for the naming rights to a stadium that hosted a Grateful Dead Fare Thee Well Tour concert for 83,000 people. The stadium is a Roman coliseum of the 21st century, green to the hilt with recycled water in the toilets and irrigation systems, solar roofs, and monitoring systems galore. Stadium nicknames include 'The Jeanhole' and 'The Big Bell Bottom.'

The stadium is an occasional venue for the San José Earthquakes soccer team. It was the site of the PAC 12 Football Championship game and Super Bowl 50 in 2016, and it has hosted events ranging from wedding fairs and monster truck jams to concerts by Jay-Z and Beyoncé and the like.

But most importantly, the stadium is home to the San Francisco 49ers, the once greats of the National Football Leagues' Western Conference. Between 1982 and 1995, the 49ers won five Super Bowls and defined a Periclean age for Bay Area sports. It was the era of Jerry Rice, Ronnie Lott, Roger Craig, Coach Bill Walsh, and of course Joe Montana.

But then for no clear reason, fan loyalty in San Francisco faded. The 49ers started out in Kezar Stadium in the Haight district, moved out to the Candlestick Park in Bayview Heights, and then when the team wanted a new stadium, people in the city didn't want to pay for it. Santa Clara grabbed that loose ball in 2014.

At the stadium there's a museum with the illustrious history of the 49ers. In eleven different gallery spaces is a place where you can study Dwight Clark making 'The Catch' in 1982, which marked the beginning of a dynasty.

Address 4900 Marie P. DeBartolo Way, Santa Clara, CA 95054, +1 (415)464-93771, www.levisstadium.com | **Getting there** Bus 140, 330 to Tasman & Centennial, or Light Rail 902 to Great America | **Hours** See website for schedule | **Tip** Step into the past at Bernal-Gulnac-Joice Ranch and immerse yourself in life on the ranch over 100 years ago (372 Manila Drive, San José, CA 95119, www.sccgov.org/sites/parks/Activities/Cultural-Venues/Pages/Bernal-Gulnac-Joice-Ranch.aspx).

87 Mission Santa Clara de Asis

A Spanish mission and the Franciscan mystique

The 16th-century system of Spanish conquest of the Americas included the notion of *reducciones*, a thickening of the social sauce as it were, whereby Indian villages were summarily destroyed and the native citizens rounded up and pressed into settlements. These settlements were designed to look like Spanish villages.

But in Alta California, 270 years later, the Franciscans recast the process of *reducciones* toward more voluntary inclusion. There was some success thanks partly to an unexpected consequence: as the conquerors infused the missions with European livestock, ranching techniques, and various technologies, small game disappeared and other foods as well, which forced the Indians to become more dependent upon the friars. As a result, hunters and gatherers became agrarian, and tribal identities were sublimated to the mixed identities in the Mission.

Such was the situation in the Santa Clara Valley in mid-January 1777, when the Franciscans founded the eighth mission of 21 in California and named it Mission Santa Clara de Thamien. The Thamien were an Ohlone tribe. Clare of Assisi had been a wealthy young Italian who devoted her life to the church.

The mission chapel has been ravaged by earthquakes and fires and rebuilt six times. In 1850, the Franciscans, then penniless, turned over the mission and the surrounding properties to Jesuits, who promptly transformed the mission into a college, now Santa Clara University, considered the West Coast's oldest operating institution of higher education. The present mission features a single bell tower, which is what it had in 1825. The chapel is open to visitors each day and well worth a visit. You can delve deeper into the mission's history at the university's de Saisset Museum.

Address 500 El Camino Real, Santa Clara, CA 95053, +1 (408)554-4000, www.scu.edu/missionchurch | Getting there Train to Santa Clara | Hours Daily 7am–dusk | Tip Visit the Children's Discovery Museum with colorful and exciting interactive learning experiences (180 Woz Way, San José, CA 95110, www.cdm.org).

88 Santa Clara Railroad Depot

History on the rails

The idea of connecting the South Bay to San Francisco with a railway came up in the 1850s, and 10 years later, several towns along the route joined together to finance the project. In 1863, the Santa Clara Railroad Depot was built and then expanded and moved around, and finally finished in 1877. It remains the oldest operating station in the state and became a vital part of an agricultural infrastructure that allowed fresh fruit to be shipped across the country.

Indeed, there was so much activity in Santa Clara that the depot featured a tower allowing for traffic control in the yards. In 1927, an 'interlocking machine' was installed in the depot and in effect became Silicon Valley's first computer. It was operational until 1993. The depot itself was acquired by Caltrans in 1980 and since 1985 has been gradually restored in large part thanks to the South Bay Historical Railroad Society, which has created one of the state's great railway museums.

The museum includes a library and period rooms, a freight receiving room, and a passenger waiting depot, with exhibits and photographs. There are references to those African Americans who became cooks, waiters, and porters and did so much to help build the black middle class in America and further the Civil Rights Movement.

The museum also features one of the largest model railroad tableaus in Northern California. Mostly N scale and HO are included in the exhibit, which fills up a large room. The scenes are tuned to the late 1950s and include replicas of famous places including packing plants, a lumber mill, and the California mission at San Miguel. The exhibit is open on Tuesdays and Saturdays only and is maintained and expanded by volunteers from the Historical Railway Society. One member told us he first came to see the trains when he was six and has been a member of the society since he was 16. He's now 32.

Address 1005 Railroad Avenue, Santa Clara, CA 95050, +1 (408) 243-3969, sbhrs.org | Getting there Caltrain to Santa Clara | Hours Tue 5–8pm, Sat 10am–3pm | Tip Visit Santa Clara's oldest adobe structure, Berryessa Adobe, built in the 1840s by one of the first colonists to settle the area (373 Jefferson Street, Santa Clara, CA 95050, www.santaclaraca.gov/Home/Components/ServiceDirectory/ServiceDirectory/121/2660).

89_ Triton Art Museum

A horseman's dream

W. Robert Morgan was a lawyer, horse rancher, and, later in life, a devotee of the arts. In 1965, in San José, he and his wife founded the Triton Art Museum, named after his favorite horse, Triton. The horse was immortalized in a 1,000-pound, life-sized bronze sculpted by Alexandrovich Schnittmann. Triton, mane flying, has stood heroically outside the museum since 1966, save the night in 1985 when pranksters from the local high school tore the horse off its pedestal and tried to carry it away, causing substantial damage to the piece.

The museum was eventually moved from San José to Santa Clara, just across the street from city government offices, and next to the performing arts center used by the Santa Clara Players. The museum is a little-known gem in the valley. The permanent collection includes such acclaimed local and regional artists as Randall Shiroma, Vicki Walsh, Lucas Blok, Doug Glovaski, and Deborah Oropallo. In recent years it has held exhibitions of work by Jennifer Sturgill, winner of the museum's 2017 Statewide Competition and Exhibition, mixed media artist Beverly Rayner, Silvia Poloto, and surrealist Eduardo Carrillo. The museum is also renowned for its bronze sculpture garden, and includes works by Sharon Loper, among others.

On the museum grounds, you will also find the historic Jamison-Brown House, a two-story home built in 1866 in the vernacular Italianate style. The house was home to several prominent San José families. One local myth is that the veranda, which was taken from another famous house called New Park, was the site where Jack London, who actually was friends with the owner, wrote much of *Call of the Wild*. The house features more than 100 different kinds of wood, including such rarities as zebra wood, Brazilian rosewood, Burma ironwood, and Cuban mahogany. Check the website for enticing events at the museum.

Address 1505 Warburton Avenue, Santa Clara, CA 95050, +1 (408)247-2438, www.tritonmuseum.org/index.php | Getting there Bus 22 to El Camino & Lincoln, or bus 32, 60 to Monroe & Warburton | Hours Tue–Sun 11am–5pm | Tip Visit the peaceful Mission Garden located behind the historic Mission Santa Clara de Asis at Santa Clara University (500 El Camino Real, Santa Clara, CA 95053, www.university-operations.scu.edu/facilities/space-data/grounds-information/mission-gardens).

90___The Mystery Spot
Tilting towards the bizarre

Among the categories of roadside attractions in America is the Tilt House, which can be traced to a Scottish geologist and physicist named John Lister, who bought an unusual property in Southern Oregon. He named it The Oregon Vortex because of gravitational anomalies in the area and opened it to the public in 1930. He spent years doing thousands of experiments but then, shortly before his death in 1959, burned all his research. No one seems to know why.

The success of The Oregon Vortex drew the interest of George Prather, an auto mechanic and science buff from Fresno who found a similarly perplexing property in the redwood forest three miles north of Santa Cruz. He had originally intended to build a home on the spot but changed his mind after he and surveyors experienced dizziness in a particular spot about 150 feet in diameter. Hand compasses also became inaccurate. And one other thing: these gravity spots seem to deter wildlife.

Prather gave up hope of a home and recast the place as a Tilt House roadside attraction, which his son opened in 1941, and which became popular after World War II as people took to the open road. Explanations for the magnetic mysteries at the Mystery Spot include a buried UFO guidance system, meteorites, a magma vortex, and a hole in the ozone layer.

As for the optical illusions, the place is indeed bizarre. Streams and balls appear to roll uphill. People leaning at absurd angles don't fall over. You appear to change height relative to others standing nearby. The core of the illusion is an old cabin set at a 20-degree angle. Add the slant of the house and the slope of a hill and you create the requirements for the illusions. The Mystery Spot is both touristy kitsch and genuine novelty. The experience includes a 45-minute guided tour, and afterwards you can take a 30-minute hike up a nearby hill. Don't miss the dahlia garden.

Address 465 Mystery Spot Road, Santa Cruz, CA 95065, +1 (831)423-8897, www.mysteryspot.com | Getting there By car, take CA-17 to Scotts Valley Drive to exit 5 to Scotts Valley Drive/Granite Creek Road. Drive 4.4 miles on Granite Creek Road. | Hours Mon–Thu 10am–4pm, Fri 9am–4pm, Sat & Sun 9am–5pm | Tip Not far away is the Scandinavian Cultural Center of Santa Cruz, where you can enjoy *jul* dinners, learn about the lives of Viking women, and much more (240 Plymouth Street, Santa Cruz, CA 95060, www.scc-santacruz.org).

91__Santa Cruz Surf Museum

Out of the valley and into the deep

On the coastal side of the mountain range that serves as the western perimeter of Santa Clara Valley, a culture thrives that would seem in direct contrast to Silicon Valley empires but is oddly resonant. You'll find it at the end of a scenic yet notoriously dangerous drive up and over Highway 17, winding through the redwoods, down to the beach-bum culture of Santa Cruz.

Santa Cruz is Ground Zero for the birth of surfing in America, and you'll find this history in the Mark Abbott Memorial Lighthouse at the Surf Museum on West Cliff Drive at Lighthouse Point. The museum is small and closely chronicles the region's role as an ongoing center of surfer culture. It all started on a summer day in 1885 – 30 years before Duke Kahanamoku popularized surfing in mainland United States – when three Hawaiian princes, who were attending boarding school in nearby San Mateo, surfed here near the mouth of the San Lorenzo River. They used 15-foot-long olo boards made of first-growth redwood trees from the nearby mountains and milled by the Grover Lumber Company. The long-board design was reserved for royalty. A facsimile of one of the boards is housed in the museum, along with a chronological board collection showing the development of materials and designs. The surfing wetsuit was also perfected here by Jack O'Neill, a local legend. Among O'Neill memorabilia on the display is an original wetsuit and many historic photographs.

The museum on Lighthouse Point overlooks the famous break known as Steamer Lane, and the surrounding coastline was recently designated a World Surfing Reserve, a status that protects the area from development that would interfere with access. Only three other places in the world, Malibu, Ericeira in Portugal, and Manly Beach in Australia, enjoy the same distinction. The museum is close to surfing equipment rental stores.

Address Lighthouse Point, 701 West Cliff Drive, Santa Cruz, CA 95060, +1 (831)420-6289, www.cityofsantacruz.com/government/city-departments/parks-recreation/facilities/ surfing-museum | **Getting there** From San José Diridon station, take bus 17 to Santa Cruz Metro Center. Change to bus 20 to Bay & West Cliff Drive. Walk 0.7 miles. | **Hours** See website for seasonal hours | **Tip** In front of Dream Inn, a beachfront hotel and the site of the first O'Neill retail store in 1959, 'Surf Shop' is the mural of porcelain-coated steel that features archival photographs of milestones in O'Neill's personal history (175 West Cliff Drive, Santa Cruz, CA 95060).

92 Seymour Marine Discovery Center

All things oceanic

The University of California at Santa Cruz campus overlooks Monterey Bay. The school is well known for its Department of Marine Biology, which is centered at the Institute of Marine Sciences. The institute opened in 1972 and does research on broad topics, like ocean processes and mammal physiology.

The institute's great advantage is its proximity to the bay, which includes the one-mile-deep Monterey Canyon. It's the largest such canyon along the West Coast of the North American continent, as deep as the Grand Canyon, and, as you can imagine, an oceanic universe of marine systems, made all the richer by the constant infusion of nutrients. Interestingly, a canyon like this would normally be formed in part by the outflows of a large river. But there is no large river here, at least not in recent geologic time.

The Institute of Marine Sciences includes both the Joseph M. Long Marine Laboratory and the Seymour Marine Discovery Center. The latter is perched on the far western cliffs of Santa Cruz and is distinguished by an 87-foot-long blue whale skeleton. The creature died in 1979 and washed ashore north of Santa Cruz on the beach in Pescadero. It may be the largest blue whale skeleton on display in the world.

Other exhibits at the center include an aquarium and a 'petting tank,' where you can examine and touch urchins, crabs, starfish, and anemones, and even a small swell shark, which is noted for its ability to inflate its stomach with water. Additional tanks include eels and jellyfish. And the center has opened up an area long held private, which is a tour of the Long Marina Laboratory, where you can see the marine mammal pools with dolphins and sea lions. Outside the center, there's a whole other world to explore with salt-water wetlands, coastal scrub, and dunes, along with many species of migratory birds.

Address 100 McAllister Way, Santa Cruz, CA 95060, +1 (831)459-3800, seymourcenter.ucsc.edu | Getting there Bus 3, 22 to Long Marine Lab & Seymour Center | Hours Tue–Sun 10am–5pm | Tip A hotspot to see monarch butterfly migrations is the Natural Bridges State Beach, where you can also admire the natural bridge across the beach (2531 West Cliff Drive, Santa Cruz, CA 95060).

93_Hakone Gardens
Natural but not wild

Japanese gardens have become increasingly popular in Silicon Valley, perhaps a reflection of the 130-year-old Japanese presence on the peninsula, but also of the growing business détente between Japanese and American venture capitalists. The startup spirit has been slow to catch on in Japan, where CEOs tend to value order and loyalty above disruption and innovation. But the pace is quickening.

In 2004, Oracle founder Larry Ellison unveiled his replica of a 16th-century Japanese emperor's palace, set on 23 acres in Woodside and now valued at approximately $70 million. Ellison might be described as a serial house-philanderer – buying up one dream house after another, never living in one for long, and then leaving them to become another museum for his art collection. The Woodside estate drew attention to Japanese architecture and landscaping.

Ellison's gardens are hidden, but you can see another very fine Japanese garden to the south, on a hillside in Saratoga. It's called the Hakone Gardens and was the dream of Isabel Stine, the wife of a real estate developer in 1915. Following the Pan-Pacific Exhibition that year, Isabel became a Japanophile, and in 1917 she traveled to the country to see Japanese historic garden sites and estates. She returned to America and built her own. The gardens were designed by Naoharu Aihara, a distinguished architect from a long line of imperial gardeners specializing in 'hill-and-pond style.' The house was eventually sold from one family to another and is now owned by the City of Saratoga.

Hakone's design follows classic principles, including miniaturization (rocks may represent mountains, and ponds represent seas), concealment (landscapes are revealed gradually), and asymmetry, whereby the garden is oriented more to scenes than features. The goal is to respect the notion that a garden should seem to be natural but not wild.

Address 21000 Big Basin Way, Saratoga, CA 95070, +1 (408)741-4994, www.hakone.com/main.html, giftshop@hakone.com | Getting there By car, take CA-85 to Saratoga Avenue, follow to destination | Hours See website for seasonal hours | Tip Continue on the road two miles west to Sanborn County Park with towering redwood trees and cool shade, a perfect place for hiking or picnicking (16055 Sanborn Road, Saratoga, CA 95070, www.sccgov.org/sites/parks/parkfinder/Pages/Sanborn.aspx).

94 Montalvo Arts Center

Califia's magical kingdom

In the 16th century, Spanish writer Garci Ordoñez de Montalvo wrote of an island rich with gold, where residents rode about on griffons and were ruled by an Amazon queen named Califia. Her kingdom was called California. At the turn of the 20th century, James Phelan was a high-profile politician in Northern California, a nativist, a mayor of San Francisco, and a US senator. When he built his Italianate mansion in Saratoga in 1912, he christened it Villa Montalvo.

On his death in 1930, Phelan willed Villa Montalvo to Santa Clara County with the directive that the estate be used to support the arts and the surrounding grounds be a public park. One of the special aspects of Montalvo, which suggests the grounds of an exclusive college, is the juxtaposition of the wild and the civilized. Visitors can enjoy miles of hiking trails through redwood forests and exotic hillside gardens, or linger in the formal Italian garden where rows of cypress frame a walkway leading to the grand lawn of the mansion. In summer months white roses bloom in profusion, while porticoed pavilions offer benches and shade. Through the 'Arts on the Grounds' project, installations and sculptures appear along the trails and walkways. A popular piece is *Curiosity Fieldstation* by Trena Noval and Ann Wettrich, a sort of naturalist office for visitors with collecting jars, and labels, shelves for displaying new specimens, and a large blackboard inviting commentary.

The artist's residency begun here in 1939 is one of the oldest in the country, and on the last Friday of the month, residents give public talks or performances in the 1,400-seat amphitheater. Visitors will find a full schedule of musical concerts and theatrical performances. The concert series here is one of the South Bay's most popular. Access to the estate is free; information about the concert series is online.

Address 15400 Montalvo Road, Saratoga, CA 95071, +1 (408)961-5800, www.montalvoarts.org | **Getting there** By car, take Highway 9 / Saratoga-Los Gatos Road. Drive 1/3 mile and turn right onto Montalvo Road. Continue approximately 1 mile to Montalvo grounds. | **Hours** Box Office, Mon–Fri 10am–4pm; see website for seasonal park hours | **Tip** To enjoy more contemporary art and local history, stop by at NUMU-New Museum Los Gatos, located just a couple of miles away (106 East Main Street, Los Gatos, CA 95030, www.numulosgatos.org).

95__ The Mountain Winery

The rise and fall of the 'Champagne King'

In 1852, Frenchman Etienne Thee goes into the wine business with a neighbor, another Frenchman, Charles LeFranc. They open a vineyard in Almaden Valley. In 1857, LeFranc marries Thee's daughter Marie Adele, and they have three children, including Henry and Louise. Henry gets run over by a trolley. Louise marries Charles LeFranc's collaborator and dashing entrepreneur, Paul Masson. Charles LeFranc dies in 1887, and a year later the family renames their business the LeFranc Masson Wine Company. Masson and his wife step into San Francisco society and become convinced that the city demands a locally grown champagne.

At the turn of the century, Masson wins recognition for his champagne and becomes known as the Champagne King. In 1905, he builds a fabulous chateau above Saratoga, his "vineyard in the sky." And so begins the bubbly years for Paul Masson. But then in 1919 comes Prohibition – the business falters and barely survives. By 1933, Masson finds himself caught in the Depression, a widower, broke, and demoralized. He sells his beloved vineyards. The buyer keeps the Masson name, and seven years later, in 1940, at 82 and often seen wandering around his old vineyards, Paul Masson dies. He's buried at Oak Hill Memorial Park in San José.

Renamed the Mountain Winery, the vineyard is on the National Register of Historic Places and has had a parade of owners. It stopped wine production in 1952 but restarted in 2004. The wine has never been able to escape its image as a demimonde label, particularly after Orson Welles, one of America's greatest filmmakers, became the brand's celebrity spokesperson but then on a talk show admitted he didn't drink the wine. The winery has become a popular venue for weddings, events, and concerts. Concert fare (May through August) includes the likes of Jethro Tull, Chris Isaak, Ziggy Marley, and Tom Jones. The view is spectacular.

Address 14831 Pierce Road, Saratoga, CA 95070, +1 (408)741-2822, www.mountainwinery.com | **Getting there** By car, take I-280 to the Foothill Expressway exit and merge onto Foothills Boulevard. Drive onto Stevens Canyon Road and straight to Mount Eden Road. Right onto Pierce Road. | **Hours** See website for hours and events | **Tip** On the way to the winery, stop by Quarry Park, originally a copper mine and then a quarry, with descriptions of the mining activity in Saratoga (22000 Congress Springs Road, Saratoga, CA 95070, www.saratoga.ca.us/Facilities/Facility/Details/Quarry-Park-11).

96 Land of Medicine Buddha
A Buddhist pilgrimage in California

Since 1852, when Chinese immigrants first opened a Buddhist temple in San Francisco's Chinatown, the Bay Area has been a place for Buddhist thought in America. From Spirit Rock in Marin County to Tassajara near Monterey, retreat centers, monasteries, and temples abound. Land of Medicine Buddha, a 'Center for Healing and Developing a Good Heart,' is nestled in the foothills of the Santa Cruz Mountains and has been welcoming visitors since 1991.

First used by Tibetan Buddhist students in the early 1980s, when the center was still an old resort known as Greenwood Lodge, it was the destruction caused by the earthquake in 1989 that made it possible for Buddhists to buy and later develop a center on the 108 acres of land. Unseen forces were obviously at work here. Today, Land of Medicine Buddha, part of the Foundation for Preservation of the Mahayana Tradition, is a beloved landmark among locals.

The center welcomes the public on to its redwood-forested trails for contemplative walking, meditation, or simply to view the many Buddhist monuments and statues. Visiting here can be like a compressed version of a Buddhist pilgrimage to India or Nepal. Near the entrance is the Great Prayer Wheel, a cylindrical drum that contains thousands of mantras, or prayers, that are thought to be activated when the wheel is turned.

A loop trail takes visitors up to a meadow with a small-scale replica of the Mahabodhi Temple, the monument in Bodh Gaya India, which marks the Buddha's place of enlightenment. Another trail, the Eight Verses Pilgrimage Loop, leads to a series of stations with placards bearing verses on transforming difficulty in spiritual practice, along with comfortable benches on which to contemplate their meaning. There are stupas and Buddha statues. And lest we forget this is California, you can, of course, find a pool and a sauna, and book a massage in advance.

Address 5800 Prescott Road, Soquel, CA 95073, +1 (831)426-8383, www.landofmedicinebuddha.org, office@medicinebuddha.org | **Getting there** By car, take CA-17 to exit 1B. Follow CA-1 S to Bay Avenue, then take exit 437 onto South Main Street to Prescott Road. | **Hours** Daily 10am–5pm | **Tip** Take a look at a very odd piece of architecture in Santa Cruz. In 1946, Kenneth Kitchen designed and built the Red Brick Castle, an abalone-inlaid brick temple known as the Court of Mysteries (519 Fair Avenue, Santa Cruz, CA 95060, www.redbrickcastle.com).

97 __Arizona Cactus Garden
Botany of desires

While today's college students are more likely to meet online than on a winding pathway, gardens were once the ideal spot for meeting and greeting. The exotic, and one might even say erotic, cacti and succulents in the Cactus Garden at Stanford University once formed the backdrop to many a co-ed romance. So common were garden trysts that the setting even found its way into a university song. Today, the garden remains a popular spot for engagement and wedding photos.

The garden was created in 1881 by the German landscape designer Rudolf Ulrich who specialized in what was then called the Arizona garden. Ulrich's signature was the use of diverse specimens and velvety turf, along with statuary and urns, artificial lakes, and hedges. He was commissioned to design the Cactus Garden for Leland and Jane Stanford who were beginning to construct their home in Palo Alto. But when their son, Leland Jr., died of typhoid fever in 1884 during a tour of Europe (see ch. 98), they scrapped plans for the house and built the university instead. The garden remained. Recently restored after long periods of neglect, the garden comes alive with brilliant scarlet and fuchsia-colored blooms.

Unique to the garden is the advanced age of many of the plants, some of which have been allowed to grow to monstrous dimensions. The ancient and robust fan palms at the entrance give the garden a decidedly tropical feel. There are more than 500 species of succulents and cacti here, including the broad variety of agaves, aloes, barrel chollas, prickly pear, and a rare Boojum tree. The garden incorporates plants, not just from Arizona but also from many of the deserts of the world; one has the sense of traveling a great distance within the small circumference of the garden. Free and open to the public every day, the Cactus Garden is a true oasis of beauty and romance.

Address Stanford University, Quarry Road, Stanford, CA 94305, www.lbre.stanford.edu/bgm/what-we-do/grounds-services/horticulture-and-landscape/points-interest/arizona-garden | Getting there Caltrain to Palo Alto | Hours Mon–Sat 10am–6pm | Tip One hundred yards away is the Stanford Mausoleum, guarded by the heartbreaking Angel of Grief, where Leland, Jane, and Leland Stanford Jr. are buried (Stanford Mausoleum, Palo Alto, CA 94304, founders.stanford.edu/stanford-history).

98__ Cantor Arts Center
The legacy of Leland Junior

In the spring of 1868, Leland and Jane Stanford were riding the wind. He was at the top of his career, having been the governor, a US senator, and one of the great investors of the day. His part of the transcontinental railway was also nearing completion. But he and his wife's greatest joy that May was the birth of Leland Jr. after 18 years of trying. Leland was then 44, Jane, 40. Leland was so delirious he arranged a dinner at their home in Sacramento, and when everyone was seated a large silver platter with a cover was brought in. Leland stood up saying he wanted to introduce someone. The cover was removed and there was a baby lying on rose blossoms.

Such was the conception of Stanford University. On a grand tour of Europe, 15 years later, Leland Junior caught typhoid and died in Florence. His parents were all but destroyed.

In 1891, as a benefit to all the Lelands of the world, they established the Leland Stanford Junior University, popularly known as Stanford, and three years later opened the Leland Stanford Junior Museum, which quickly acquired a worldwide reputation. But then two earthquakes in 83 years caused terrible damage. It wasn't until 1999 that a completely refurbished museum opened: The Iris & B. Gerald Cantor Center for Visual Arts.

The center, with 24 galleries, is known for its Native American collection; its works by post-World War II American artists, such as Pollock, Rothko, Reinhardt, and de Kooning; and, above all, for the Auguste Rodin collection, the largest outside France. But in one out-of-the-way gallery, you'll come across three drawings by Leland, Jr. Two are of a house and a tree, another of a horse and groom. The drawings are remarkable for someone about 12 years of age, less because of the subject and the advanced but subtle style, than for the extraordinary care with which they were done. It's remarkable to think that we owe so much of today's technology innovations to this boy's untimely death.

Address 28 Lomita Drive at Museum Way, Stanford, CA 94305, +1 (650)723-4177, museum.stanford.edu | **Getting there** Bus N, P, X-Exp to Roth @ Cantor Arts | **Hours** Mon, Wed, Fri 11am–5pm, Thu 11am–8pm | **Tip** Adjacent to Cantor Arts Center, is the Anderson Collection, which houses one of the best private collections of modern and contemporary American art (314 Lomita Drive, Stanford, CA 94305, anderson.stanford.edu).

99 Dymaxion Chronofile
The life of a random element

Buckminster Fuller (1885–1983) once described himself as a "random element." He also described himself as a "comprehensive, anticipatory design scientist." Colleagues imagined him as a polymath. The truth is he cannot be adequately described. He was a genius and a crackpot. He was a philosopher and an architect, and a bit of a Howard Roark character. He was an American da Vinci, a human brainstorm. He once gave an 18-hour lecture.

When he stepped out on a stage, to some he appeared – in contrast to his intellectual stare – as a "small shopkeeper from New England," which is where he grew up. His father died when 'Bucky' was young. The son was a know-it-all in school and a bully, and he was thrown out of Harvard twice, once for "general irresponsibility." "Whenever I draw a circle," he once said, "I immediately want to step out of it."

He went through towering success and utter failure. Not to mention holding his three-year-old daughter in his arms as she died from spinal meningitis. Nevertheless, he did what all great creatives do – he kept going. He once described himself as a "verb." He felt he didn't belong to himself but to humankind. He was obsessed by the prospects for humanity in an age of science. He was convinced that science and technology could solve any problem. He believed the whole universe is intention.

He is best known for his Dymaxion creations, the word derived from the first letters of 'dynamic, maximum, and tension,' which was the foundation of his thesis: "Maximum gain of advantage from minimal energy input." And so the Dymaxion car, house, map, and Chronofile. The latter was a scrapbook of Fuller's life, a case study of social evolution, kept from 1920 to 1983, with the idea that he would add something every 15 minutes. You can view the Chronofile of this amazing man at the Buckminster Fuller Archive at Stanford University Library.

Address Stanford University Libraries, 557 Escondido Mall, Stanford, CA 94305, library.stanford.edu/collections/r-buckminster-fuller-collection | Getting there Bus C, C-LIM to Serra Mall & Hoover Tower, or Serra Mall & Mem Aud | Hours Daily 9am – 5pm; The Dymaxion Chronofile is part of the Libraries' Department of Special Collections and it requires an individual request access two days prior to arrival. | Tip Visit the Papua New Guinea Sculpture Garden, which is hidden in a small wooded area of Stanford University. It contains stone and wooden artworks sculpted by a group of artisans from the Sepik region of Papua New Guinea (Santa Teresa Street & Lomita Drive, Stanford, CA 94305).

100___Hanna Honeycomb House

The power of the hive

Innovation is woven into the design of Silicon Valley, in ways big and small, and often the most radical concepts grow from a subtle shift in perspective. In Frank Lloyd Wright's Hanna Honeycomb House, opening the 90-degree angle to 120 degrees released a swarm of architectural developments that continue to resonate through architecture today. Built in 1937 for Stanford professors Paul and Jean Hanna, the design is based on the geometry of the hexagon. The result, with un-cornered rooms, establishes a unique sense of openness that allows for the free flow of movement from space to space. The design is considered a breakthrough in Wright's career and lead, however indirectly, to his work on the Guggenheim Museum in Manhattan. It's his first design based on non-rectangular forms.

Built of red San José brick and native redwood, Hanna House 'completes the hillside' in architectural parlance, referring to the organic relationship between the house and the contours of the hill on which it's built. Moreover, because there are no right angles in the house, the hexagonal motif is carried through the exterior floor plan as well as the interior finishes. Tiles, floor patterns, and the original furniture all echo the hexagonal hive theme.

It was Wright's first residence on the West Coast and is unique in that Wright worked with the Hanna family to expand the house as their family grew. Long recognized as an architectural landmark, the house was given to Stanford by the family in 1975 and was used to house the university provosts until 1989, when the house, along with other major structures on the Stanford Campus, was badly damaged in the Loma Prieta earthquake. The house was built on the San Andreas Fault, and Wright knew that. The house is open to the public, although you need to book well in advance.

Address 737 Frenchman's Road, Stanford, CA 94305, +1 (650)725-8352, www.hannahousetours.stanford.edu, hannahouse@stanford.edu | Getting there By car, follow Campus Drive in Stanford University and turn south onto Mayfield Avenue, then left on Frenchman's Road | Hours See website to schedule a visit | Tip Another Frank Lloyd Wright house in Silicon Valley is Arthur Mathews House in Atherton, with a diamond-shaped floor plan (83 Wisteria Way, Atherton, CA 94027, www.franklloydwrightsites.com/california/mathews/mathews_house.html).

101 Hoover Tower

Stunning views of the past

Herbert Hoover (1874–1964) was the nation's 31st president, a Republican from New York. He was a savvy businessman with a reputation for honesty and sound management skills, although ultimately poor judgment, notably his support of the Smoot-Hawley Tariff, which in 1930 caused trade wars and, in the view of many historians, exacerbated the Great Depression. Hoover was withdrawn, extremely sensitive to criticism, and a poor communicator. He's seen more favorably for what he did before and after his presidency, particularly the historical archives he gave to Stanford University in 1919. He was in the pioneer class of 1895.

The archives are held in the Hoover Institution on War, Revolution, and Peace on the Stanford campus. The institution is a conservative think tank; the archives contain 5,000 individual collections and documents spanning almost all of 20th-century history. They were originally imagined as a record of World War I but gradually encompassed the political currents in the interwar period through the end of World War II and beyond. They also reflect Hoover's particular interests in humanitarian relief and Soviet/Russian politics. The material is kept in 100,000 boxes and made available for use in the Hoover Institution Archives reading room. See the loan desk in the first floor of the Hoover Tower.

You can visit the top of the 285-foot Hoover Tower. It's $2 for a 360-degree view. The art deco tower, finished in 1941, was designed by Arthur Brown Jr., who also designed the Coit Tower in San Francisco, inspired by the cathedral tower in Salamanca, Spain. The top three stories are offices, the first nine floors are for the stacks. In the mid-1970s, Aleksandr Solzhenitsyn lived on the 11th floor. The tower is also known for its carillon of 48 bells on the 14th floor. Note also a very touching exhibit on the life of First Lady Lou Henry Hoover.

Address 550 Serra Mall, Stanford, CA 94305, +1 (650)723-2053, www.visit.stanford.edu/plan/guides/hoover.html | Getting there Bus C, C-LIM, SLAC to Serra Mall @ Villa Ortega, bus O, SE to Campus @ Cogen LKSC, or bus SLAC, X, X-LIM to Via Ortega & Cypress Lot | Hours Daily 10am–4pm | Tip To experience all-inclusive luxury, book a room at the Clement Hotel, a boutique hotel with a rooftop pool just across from Stanford University (711 El Camino Real, Palo Alto, CA 94301, www.theclementpaloalto.com).

102_ The Red Barn at Stanford
Movies & moving horses

Stanford University's nickname 'The Farm' has a ring of irony these days, considering the high-tech science for which the school is most famous. But in 1879, the land really was a stock farm, overseen by governor millionaire Leland Stanford, an enthusiastic hobbyist of trotting horses. The farm, where Stanford bred and raised over 600 horses, included 50 paddocks and 8 tracks. At the center of the farm was, and is, a vast Victorian-style barn, painted red and lined with palm trees. The Red Barn is one of the oldest buildings on campus and houses the Stanford Equestrian team, as well as several community equestrian programs. But none of that is why it's famous.

Eager to be taken seriously as a horse expert, Stanford had a theory that in the gait of a trotting horse there was a moment when all of the animal's hooves were airborne at the same time. The theory was difficult to prove. Photography, still a fledgling art, lacked the quick exposures we now take for granted, which is where photographer Eadweard Muybridge comes in. Muybridge worked out an elaborate course in front of the Red Barn, where a system of trip wires, multiple exposures, and special emulsion plates, captured the gait of a trotting horse. The result was a series of consecutive images. Stanford, as it turned out, was right. Horses do fly.

Muybridge recognized in this system of sequential exposures the potential to record movement in new ways. He created a way to project the images of the horses via the 'zoopraxiscope' onto a screen. He gave a public viewing in San Francisco in 1879. Moving pictures were on their way. Repeating the techniques perfected at the Red Barn, Muybridge went on to photograph humans and other animals, revealing the anatomy of motion for the first time. The 'dictionary of movement' he created remains a standard reference for artists and designers.

Address 100 Electioneer Road, Stanford, CA 94305, +1 (650)327-2990, web.stanford.edu/group/sct/cgi-bin/wordpress/facilities-boarding | **Getting there** Bus O, OCA, SE, SLAC to Santa Teresa @ Arboles | **Hours** Daily dawn–dusk | **Tip** Take a self-guided tour of plants, animals, and science art on Stanford Campus (web.stanford.edu/group/stanfordbirds/SciArtPodcast/Sci_Art_Nat_Walk_Podcast.html).

103 — Stanford Memorial Church

Nondenominational jewel

Frederick Law Olmsted was a preeminent landscape designer, as well as farmer and journalist, whose works include Central Park in Manhattan and the master plan for Stanford University. As you drive into the heart of Stanford underneath Canary Island palms, you may notice the brilliant golden glow coming from the Stanford Memorial Church. The glow comes off the reflection of thousands of gold-infused tiles, or *tesserae*, in the mosaic on the façade.

The church was commissioned by Jane Stanford (1828–1905) as a memorial to her husband, Leland Stanford. It was intended to be "the centerpiece of the university complex."

The Stanford Memorial Church, which anchors the main quad, was finished in 1903. It was designed by Charles Coolidge in the style of Richardsonian Romanesque, which blended together 11th- and 12th-century French, Spanish, and Italian Romanesque influences. The soaring interior, decorated with majestic mosaics and topped with exposed wooden beams in a craftsman style, is different from a typical European cathedral. Among the 140 stained-glass windows throughout the church is one depicting Leland Stanford Jr. ascending to heaven. He was Leland Stanford's 15-year-old son who died of typhoid in 1884 and became the namesake of the university (see ch. 98). Characteristic of a nondenominational church, there may be a Catholic mass going on in one chapel and Zen meditation in another.

The church has a dark story attached to it though. Late on the night of October 12, 1974, Arlis Perry, a 19-year-old newlywed, went to pray in the church and was reported missing later that night by her husband, a Stanford student. She was found the next morning, murdered by the church security guard. But the murder was solved only 44 years later in 2018.

Address Building 500, 450 Serra Mall, Stanford, CA 94305, +1 (650)723-1762,
www.live.stanford.edu/plan-your-visit/venues/memorial-church | **Getting there** Bus C,
CLIM, SLAC to Serra Mall @ Oval, or Serra Mall @ Main Quad | **Hours** Mon–Fri
8am–5pm, Sun 11:30am–3:30pm | **Tip** A couple of minutes away is the lovely
Thomas Welton Stanford Art Gallery (419 Lasuen Mall, Stanford University, Stanford,
CA 94305, art.stanford.edu/exhibition-spaces/stanford-art-gallery).

104_ Libby's Water Tank

Behold the tin can

The art of preserving food in glass jars and tin cans was developed by the French in the early 1800s and then spread to England. The idea was important to generals planning military campaigns and explorers mapping out expeditions. In the mid-19th century, the British middle class also attributed a certain luxury status to canned food. The first canning factory in America opened in New York in 1812. Interestingly, in 1865 a steamboat delivering goods to the Montana territories sank in the Missouri River. No crew members were lost, but all the cargo, which included canned peaches, oysters, and plum tomatoes, was. In 1974, the cans were found, tested, and determined to be still edible, although they weren't so tasty.

Canning technology reached California in the late 1800s, about the time high taxes forced farmers to abandon wheat in favor of fruit. In 1906, the Libby, McNeill, & Libby Company, a corned-beef packing operation in Chicago, was lured to Sunnyvale by the offer of free land. This was part of a regional recovery effort following the San Francisco earthquake. The Silicon Valley of its time became known as the Garden of the World, and by 1922, Libby's was the largest cannery in the world.

Because canneries were seasonal and depended on cheap labor – hiring successive waves of Chinese, Italians, Portuguese, Japanese, and Latinos – canneries in Sunnyvale became a bellwether of food manufacturing trends. The original Libby factory closed in 1985. The space was recast as a business park, whose tenants include among others, Raytheon and Walmart Labs. Nevertheless, the 150,000-gallon water tower that had long served the cannery was preserved. It had been rebuilt in 1965 and painted by a local artist, Anita Kaplan, into a 25-foot-tall fruit can, with a 15-foot diameter, resplendent with the original Libby's insignia from the 1900s, boasting *Fancy Fruits For Salad*.

Address 490 West California Avenue, Sunnyvale, CA 94086 | **Getting there** Bus 32, 54 to California & Mathilda | **Hours** Unrestricted | **Tip** In search for peace and meditation? Visit Sunnyvale Hindu Temple and Community Center (450 Persian Drive, Sunnyvale, CA 94089, www.sunnyvale-hindutemple.org).

105 Alice's Restaurant

But not Arlo Guthrie's

Sky Londa is an unincorporated, census-designated blur of a place in the coastal mountains above Palo Alto. Sometimes spelled Skylonda, or originally, Sky L'onda, the name is a compression of Skyline Drive and La Honda. The latter is a community scattered along the western slopes of the range. While Sky Londa may be unfamiliar even to people who live in this part of the peninsula, it's well known to pilots approaching SFO from the south because of a VOR ground station in the area.

Sky Londa had been a getaway since the 1930s for San Francisco's middle-class residents, who were quick to buy up cheap logging land and build summer vacation cabins that cost $750. By 1932, there were some 60 cabins built, which have been recast into housing for Silicon Valley commuters.

Downtown Sky Londa is the intersection of Highway 35 and Highway 84. You'll find a couple of gas stations, the Skywood Trading Post, a real estate office, – where you can still find homes for less than $3 million, – and a couple of restaurants, including Alice's, which is often assumed to be the restaurant described in Arlo Guthrie's 1967 iconic song. It isn't. The real Alice's restaurant, at 40 Main Street in Stockbridge, Massachusetts, was started by Alice Brock.

Sky Londa's Alice was Alice Taylor who bought a coffee shop in the 1960s, which has become a famously popular burger and brew stop for weekend bikers of all kinds. The two parking lots are usually packed with every kind of motorcycle from flamboyant to rare: Harleys, Moto Guzzi, Ducatis, Nortons, or custom-made bikes, along with a few amazing classic cars like a Lamborghinis Miura, and a Ferrari 250 Spyder GT California parked side by side.

Alice's Restaurant has been the site of several high-profile product announcements, including the release of the 1991 Kawasaki Ninja, the 2008 Tesla, and several rare models by Ducati.

Address 17288 Skyline Boulevard, Woodside, CA 94062, +1 (650)851-0303, www.alicesrestaurant.com | Getting there Bus 85 to La Honda Road & Grandview Drive | Hours Mon–Sat 8am–9pm, Sun 8am–7pm | Tip A few miles south on La Honda Road is Apple Jack's Inn. The old roadhouse bar was built in 1879 as a blacksmith shop for passing travelers (8790 La Honda Road, La Honda, CA 94020).

106_ Clos de la Tech

On the slopes of old and new worlds

The western perimeter of Silicon Valley is roughly Route 35, which runs along the ridge of the coastal mountains between Highway 92 and Highway 17. The area includes vineyards and several small communities, with long histories and sometimes uncertain futures. La Honda, for example, is a berg on the western side of Route 35, with a population of several hundred people, – but, according to a recent census, falling dramatically.

Few towns have been home to the celebrities of alternative culture in California more than La Honda. Residents in the last 50 years include, Neil and Pegi Young, gonzo journalist Hunter S. Thompson, novelist Ken Kesey and the Merry Pranksters, Allen Ginsberg, and members of the Hell's Angels motorcycle club. Silicon Valley entrepreneurs include Reed Hastings, co-founder and CEO of Netflix, and Paul Vixie, known for his work on Domain Name Systems (DNS).

And then there's T. J. Rodgers, who got his PhD in electrical engineering from Stanford and started the Cypress Semiconductor Corporation. In 1996, 'Docteur' Rodgers opened Clos de la Tech, a biodynamic winery in La Honda consisting of caves built into a mountain ridge, along with 168 acres of vineyards, some on 35-degree slopes. The docteur's specialty is Pinot Noir, using a "Burgundian approach." He produces 1,000 cases annually, and a microchip is attached to every bottle.

Rodgers and his wife Valeta Massey have spared neither time nor money, in finding the best land, the most efficient growing techniques, and the most effective means of harvesting the grapes. The docteur helped to develop a revolutionary tractor for steep slopes. It has no motor or brakes, and it is steered using a 'joystick.' Such is the fusion of old world and tech. Although the winery is not open to the public, there's a tasting room at The Half Moon Bay Wine and Cheese Company.

Address 535 Eastview Way, Woodside, CA 94062, +1 (650)722-3038, www.closdelatech.com/article/home, info@closdelatech.com | **Getting there** By car only, take I-280 to Cañada Road. Continue to Glencrag Way and drive to Eastview Way. | **Hours** Call for a tour | **Tip** You can practice your horseback riding and archery skills nearby in Huddart Park (1100 Kings Mountain Road, Woodside, CA 94062, www.parks.smcgov.org/huddart-park).

107__Djerassi Foundation Artist Program
The art of contraception

The Djerassi Foundation's resident artists' retreat occupies a vast piece of land near Woodside. Artists from around the world come here to commune with pristine hills and endless sky, and some leave behind their artworks, which form much of the retreat's mystique. Access to the ranch is limited, the story of the Djerassi family is one of the central narratives of Silicon Valley legend.

Carl Djerassi (1923–2015) was the son of Austrian scientists who emigrated to America before World War II. Carl went on to become a prominent chemist and in 1951, working in Mexico City with two other chemists, isolated the compounds for artificial progesterone, the key to the birth-control pill. The sexual revolution that followed shaped the culture of California and the world. Djerassi became a Stanford professor in 1960 and purchased the ranch in Woodside that is now the retreat. He and his wife, along with both his daughter Pamela and son Dale, built homes on the ranch. Then, in 1978, Pamela, an artist and poet, committed suicide. She was 28. Djerassi, a prominent art collector, focused his grief on supporting the work of living artists, especially women. The ranch was converted to an artist residence and has become one of the most highly sought-after artist residencies in the world. A changing cohort of international poets, writers, dancers, and visual artists share ideas and space at Djerassi. The foundation also helps develop other arts organizations.

Among the unique programs is the Science, Delirium, Madness monthly session in which artists and scientists come together in a shared residency to foster creative dialog across disciplines. The program is a fitting memorial to the arts institution that science built! Several times throughout the year, the grounds are open to the public via the Sculpture Hikes, special events, and conferences.

Address 2325 Bear Gulch Road, Woodside, CA 94062, +1 (650)747-1250, www.djerassi.org | Getting there By car only, take CA-35 and turn south on Bear Gulch Road | Hours See website for times and book ahead | Tip On Skyline Road, between Alice's Restaurant and Skeggs Vista Point you can see the oldest and largest living redwood tree in Woodside, the giant Methuselah Tree.

108_Filoli

Flowering wealth

Among the great mansions on the San Francisco Peninsula, the largest ones include the Winchester Mystery House (see ch. 80), the Carolands Mansion (see ch. 20), and the Filoli Estate near Woodside. The last is west of Highway 280, south of the Crystal Springs Reservoir. The 650-acre property includes beautiful gardens, around the main house built in 1919 by an Irishman named Bourne. He made his money in gold mines in Grass Valley and stuck to this credo, "Fight for a just cause, love your fellow man, live a good life." Take the first two letters of each verb and you have 'Fi-lo-li.'

The place was designed as a 43-room country house in the Georgian style for people who sometimes regarded themselves as gentleman farmers. Inside the house, key rooms remain dressed to the nines. In the study, the atmosphere is filled with a scrabble game in progress, half-finished glasses of Jack Daniels, and on the shelves, books about sailing ships and thoroughbred horses. A secret door opens to one of the first bars built in a private home, a room lined with horse-themed wallpaper. It's all suggestive of an American Downton Abbey.

But the Filoli Estate is mostly renowned for its exquisite English Renaissance-style gardens, which cover 16 acres and offer a magnificent palette of colors and smells from the countless types of flowers. A variety of tree species cover an additional seven acres of land. Filoli gardens hold a place as one of the most magical gardens in Northern California.

Specialty tours include one on mushrooms and another that takes you past grazing deer, across Fault Creek, and up a narrow trail to a cemetery and a lake. The fault is the San Andreas Fault, which is the intersection of the Pacific and North American plates.

Filoli was a set for the 1980s television soap opera *Dynasty*, and it was featured in movies such as *Heaven Can Wait*, *The Joy Luck Club*, and many more.

Address 86 Cañada Road, Woodside, CA 94062, +1 (650)364-8300, www.filoli.org, tickets@filoli.org | Getting there By car only, take I-280 to exit 39 and follow Cañada Road to Filoli | Hours Tue–Sun 10am–5pm | Tip If you are in the mood for some jazz music, get tickets to the Filoli Jazz Series (filoli.org/jazz), which celebrates world-renowned jazz masters every Sunday throughout the summer.

109__Folger Stable

Happy trails to you

Among the lesser-known parks in Silicon Valley are two jewels: Huddart and Wunderlich. Huddart is named after a man, an orphan, and a lumber baron at the turn of the 19th century, who deeded 900 acres to the county for the betterment of youth. The park was home to Native Americans as recently as 1857, and you see right away what lush territory it was and still is. The terrain rises and falls with redwood and oak forests, vast meadows, streams, and chaparral. Wildlife includes black-tailed deer, bobcats, coyotes, mountain lions, and red-tailed hawks. The park, with 24 miles of trails, is located just north of Woodside, off Kings Mountain Road.

You'll find Wunderlich County Park, Huddart's sister park, a mile west of the Village Bakery on CA-84. Both are overseen by the same nonprofit organization.

Wunderlich is home to the Folger Estate Stable Historic District. The grounds include the main working stable, a dairy house, the blacksmith barn, stone walkways, and a carriage house. The architectural style is French baroque, but you'll notice aspects of the Arts and Crafts Movement. The architect was Arthur Brown Jr., who also designed San Francisco City Hall, the Opera House, and Coit Tower.

One of the tenants at Wunderlich is Chaparral, a company that offers year-round trail rides in several spots around the Bay Area. Trail rides at Wunderlich are open to adventurers eight years old and above, riding well-trained quarter horses on all-weather trails. One of their new long rides runs from the Folger Stable to Purissima Creek in Half Moon Bay. The cost is $250 per person; reservations are required. For those who have no experience riding horses but would like to try, another tenant at the Folger Stable is Alo Horses, "Spiritually Guiding Humans," which offers four-day camps directed by certified practitioners of the Equine Gestalt Coaching Method.

Address 4040 Woodside Road, Woodside, CA, 94062, +1 (650)851-1210,
www.parks.smcgov.org/wunderlich-park | Getting there By car only, take I-280 to
CA-84/Woodside Road | Hours Daily 8am–dusk | Tip To really spoil yourself, visit
the Village Bakery for a meal or simply try the baked goods (3052 Woodside Road,
Woodside, CA 94062, www.tvbwoodside.com).

110_ The Mountain House
Home of the unknown legend

One of the greatest drives in all California, particularly near the coast, is Highway 35, otherwise known as Skyline Drive. At the northern end, it starts not far from the San Francisco Zoo. But the place to pick it up is where it intersects Highway 92, above Half Moon Bay, and then runs south along the ridge of the Coast Mountains, ending up above Santa Cruz, where 35 meets Highway 17. There are points on this road where you can see both the Pacific Ocean and San Francisco Bay, and many roads drop down in either direction. There are also many trail heads. The road itself is a rally racer's fantasy, narrow and curvy. On the weekends in particular, you'll find it filled with people, some of whom are very nice people but gone quite mad on bicycles and motorcycles, shooting the rapids, as it were, down through fir forests.

There are few eateries along the route. But one of the most famous is the Mountain House Restaurant, best known for one of its customers, Neil Young, the tenor rock star, film director, and humanitarian, once called the Godfather of Grunge. Predictably unpredictable, he has always trusted in the notion that "chaos is good," which, ironically, is exactly the ethos of Silicon Valley. In the 1970s, Young bought a 140-acre ranch near La Honda. The Mountain House has served as a rendezvous point with the press over the years and was used in his 1992 video for *Unknown Legend*.

The Mountain House, hidden away in a Redwood Grove, was originally named the Kings Rendezvous after the local community called Kings Mountain. In the 1940s, it was the Red Pump, and then in the 1980s, Alex's Mountain House. It's become less funky over the years, and these days the atmosphere might be described as an upscale hunting lodge with the added glass house dining area called the Forest Room. Entrees include an elk medallion. Outside you can find a Tesla hookup.

Address 13808 Skyline Boulevard, Woodside, CA 94062, +1 (650)851-8541, www.themountainhouse.com, info@themountainhouse.com | Getting there By car, take I-280 to I-84, and follow CA-35/King Mountain Road to Skyline Boulevard | Hours Wed–Sun 5–9pm | Tip For a view of the Bay Area and even parts of San Francisco, drive the scenic route to the Russian Ridge Open Space Reserve on Skyline Boulevard at the intersection of Page Mill and Alpine Road (www.openspace.org/preserves/russian-ridge).

111__Woodside
The scent of well-heeled horses

Halfway between San Francisco and San José, across Interstate 280 from Stanford University, there's Woodside, an if-only-I-could-live-here horse town of 5,500. Among the customs, residents are advised to 'rough up' asphalt driveways and refrain from tying balloons to mailboxes. Otherwise, horses may slip or spook. The social climate is elegant and charming. Originally, the Ohlone Indians occupied the land along the eastern slopes of the Coast Range. Over more recent years, residents have included Joan Baez, Steve Jobs, and Bill Walsh, reflecting the diverse backgrounds of the people who have lived here.

There's a landmark from the 1850s on Tripp Road just beyond the town of Woodside: a time capsule with a post office just as it was, a general store, and a community gathering center, including what was then a state-of-the-art dentist chair. In the 1800s, the General Store was the center of the town where locals attended to their daily business. Now the restored building is a small museum.

The town center is focused on a short stretch of a two-lane road with a rustic downtown. You will come across The Little Store, serving French bistro food for lunch and dinner. The proprietor is from the South of France, but the interior features Western memorabilia on the walls. People who live in the city find the place particularly quaint and welcoming.

Woodside might be dismissed as merely another wealthy community, a West Coast Greenwich, but there's much more to it. Among the 25 or so local horse clubs and associations, there's the National Center for Equine Facilitated Therapy (NCEFT). The Center is a nonprofit started 45 years ago as a way to help children, veterans, and first responders suffering from disabilities. Therapy derived from the movement of the horse provides sensory input that helps facilitate "changes in sensory integration and attention skills."

Address Woodside Store, 3300 Tripp Road, Woodside, CA 94062, +1 (650)851-7615, www.woodsidetown.org | Getting there Bus 85 to Tripp Road & Woodside Road, walk 0.8 miles | Hours Woodside Store, Tue & Thu 10am–4pm, Sat & Sun noon–4pm | Tip The Pioneer Saloon is a fun place to see live music on the weekends (2925 Woodside Road, Woodside, CA 94062, www.pioneer-saloon.com).

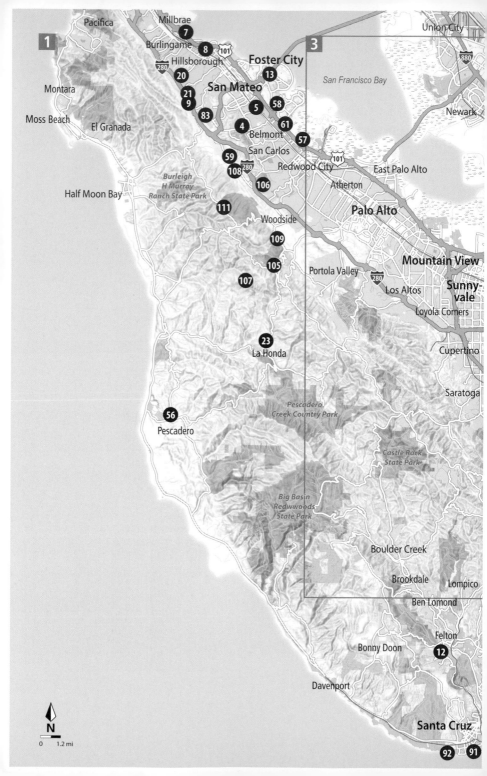

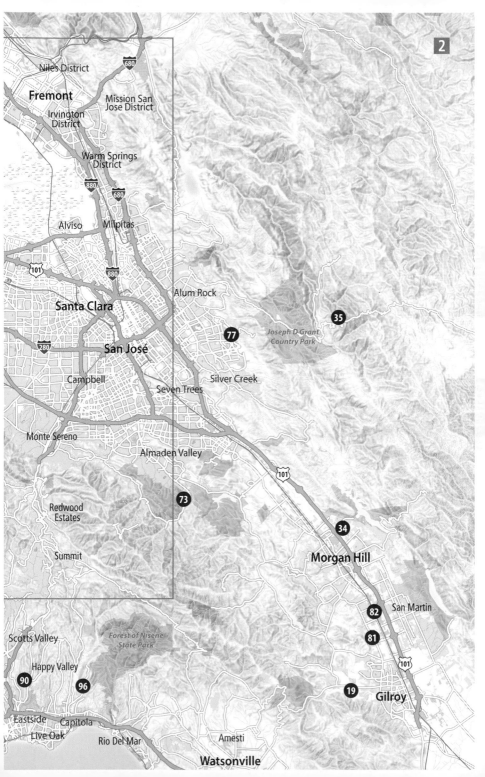

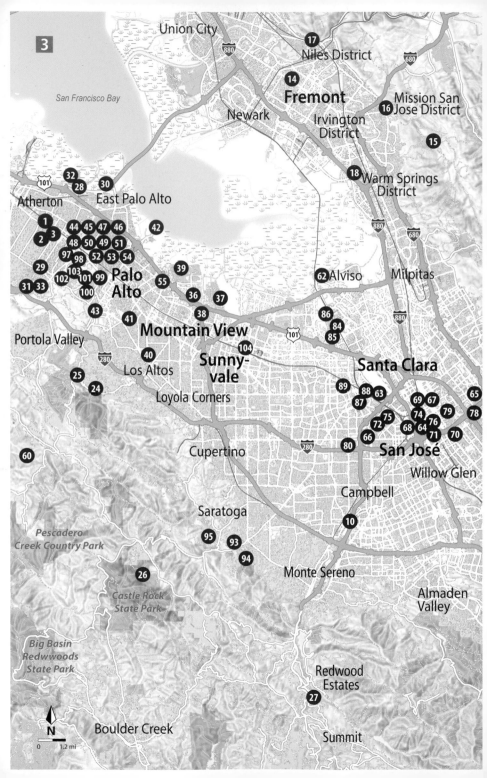

Michelle Madden, Janet McMillan
**111 Places in Milwaukee
That You Must Not Miss**
ISBN 978-3-7408-0491-6

Joe Conzo, Kevin C. Fitzpatrick
**111 Places in the Bronx
That You Must Not Miss**
ISBN 978-3-7408-0492-3

Leslie Adatto, Clay Williams
**111 Rooftops in New York
That You Must Not Miss**
ISBN 978-3-7408-0495-4

John Major, Ed Lefkowicz
**111 Places in Brooklyn
That You Must Not Miss**
ISBN 978-3-7408-0380-3

Wendy Lubovich, Ed Lefkowicz
**111 Museums in New York
That You Must Not Miss**
ISBN 978-3-7408-0379-7

Anita Mai Genua, Clare Davenport,
Elizabeth Lenell Davies
**111 Places in Toronto
That You Must Not Miss**
ISBN 978-3-7408-0257-8

Andréa Seiger
111 Places in Washington D.C.
That You Must Not Miss
ISBN 978-3-7408-0258-5

Elisabeth Larsen
111 Places in The Twin Cities
That You Must Not Miss
ISBN 978-3-7408-0029-1

Joe DiStefano, Clay Williams
111 Places in Queens
That You Must Not Miss
ISBN 978-3-7408-0020-8

Allison Robicelli, John Dean
111 Places in Baltimore
That You Must Not Miss
ISBN 978-3-7408-0158-8

Amy Bizzarri, Susie Inverso
111 Places in Chicago
That You Must Not Miss
ISBN 978-3-7408-0156-4

Laurel Moglen, Julia Posey,
Lyudmila Zotova
111 Places in Los Angeles
That You Must Not Miss
ISBN 978-3-95451-884-5

Gordon Streisand
111 Places in Miami and the Keys
That You Must Not Miss
ISBN 978-3-95451-644-5

Floriana Petersen, Steve Werney
111 Places in San Francisco
That You Must Not Miss
ISBN 978-3-95451-609-4

Jo-Anne Elikann
111 Places in New York
That You Must Not Miss
ISBN 978-3-95451-052-8

Dave Doroghy, Graeme Menzies
111 Places in Vancouver
That You Must Not Miss
ISBN 978-3-7408-0494-7

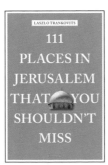

Laszlo Trankovits
111 Places in Jerusalem
That You Shouldn't Miss
ISBN 978-3-7408-0320-9

Christoph Hein, Sabine Hein
111 Places in Singapore
That You Shouldn't Miss
ISBN 978-3-7408-0382-7

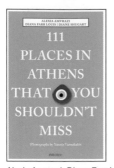

Alexia Amvrazi, Diana Farr Louis,
Diane Shugart, Yannis Varouhakis
**111 Places in Athens
That You Shouldn't Miss**
ISBN 978-3-7408-0377-3

Benjamin Haas, Leonie Friedrich
**111 Places in Buenos Aires
That You Must Not miss**
ISBN 978-3-7408-0260-8

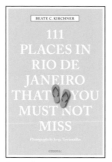

Beate C. Kirchner
**111 Places in Rio de Janeiro
That You Must Not Miss**
ISBN 978-3-7408-0262-2

Andrea Livnat, Angelika Baumgartner
**111 Places in Tel Aviv
That You Shouldn't Miss**
ISBN 978-3-7408-0263-9

Kai Oidtmann
**111 Places in Iceland
That You Shouldn't Miss**
ISBN 978-3-7408-0030-7

Christine Izeki, Björn Neumann
**111 Places in Tokyo
That You Shouldn't Miss**
ISBN 978-3-7408-0024-6